taming
the sicilian

Nigel Davies

EVERYMAN CHESS

Everyman Publishers plc   www.everymanbooks.com

First published in 2002 by Everyman Publishers plc, formerly Cadogan Books plc, Gloucester Mansions, 140A Shaftesbury Avenue, London WC2H 8HD

Copyright © 2002 Nigel Davies

The right of Nigel Davies to be identified as the author of this work has been asserted in accordance with the Copyrights, Designs and Patents Act 1988.

British Library Cataloguing-in-Publication Data
A catalogue record for this book is available from the British Library.

ISBN 1 85744 301 2

Distributed in North America by The Globe Pequot Press, P.O Box 480, 246 Goose Lane, Guilford, CT 06437-0480.

All other sales enquiries should be directed to Everyman Chess, Gloucester Mansions, 140A Shaftesbury Avenue, London WC2H 8HD
tel: 020 7539 7600 fax: 020 7379 4060
email: chess@everymanbooks.com
website: www.everymanbooks.com

To Louise and Sam

EVERYMAN CHESS SERIES (formerly Cadogan Chess)
Chief advisor: Garry Kasparov
Commissioning editor: Byron Jacobs

Typeset and edited by First Rank Publishing, Brighton.
Production by Book Production Services.
Printed and bound in Great Britain by The Cromwell Press Ltd., Trowbridge, Wiltshire.

Everyman Chess

Popular opening books:

1 85744 218 0	Unusual QG Declined	Chris Ward
1 85744 253 9	Alekhine's Defence	Nigel Davies
1 85744 256 4	Queen's Gambit Declined	Matthew Sadler
1 85744 232 6	French Classical	Byron Jacobs
1 85744 281 4	Modern Defence	Speelman & McDonald
1 85744 292 X	Symmetrical English	David Cummings
1 85744 290 3	c3 Sicilian	Joe Gallagher
1 85744 239 3	Grunfeld Defence	Nigel Davies
1 85744 242 3	Offbeat Spanish	Glenn Flear
1 85744 262 8	Classical Nimzo-Indian	Bogdan Lalic
1 85744 291 1	Sicilian Grand Prix Attack	James Plaskett
1 85744 252 0	Dutch Stonewall	Jacob Aagaard
1 85744 257 1	Sicilian Kalashnikov	Pinski & Aagaard
1 85744 276 8	French Winawer	Neil McDonald

Books for players serious about improving their game:

1 85744 226 1	Starting Out in Chess	Byron Jacobs
1 85744 231 8	Tips for Young Players	Matthew Sadler
1 85744 236 9	Improve Your Opening Play	Chris Ward
1 85744 241 5	Improve Your Middlegame Play	Andrew Kinsman
1 85744 246 6	Improve Your Endgame Play	Glenn Flear
1 85744 223 7	Mastering the Opening	Byron Jacobs
1 85744 228 8	Mastering the Middlegame	Angus Dunnington
1 85744 233 4	Mastering the Endgame	Glenn Flear
1 85744 238 5	Simple Chess	John Emms

Books for the more advanced player:

1 85744 233 4	Attacking with 1 e4	John Emms
1 85744 233 4	Attacking with 1 d4	Angus Dunnington
1 85744 219 9	Meeting 1 e4	Alexander Raetsky
1 85744 224 5	Meeting 1 d4	Aagaard and Lund
1 85744 273 3	Excelling at Chess	Jacob Aagaard

taming
the sicilian

Nigel Davies

EVERYMAN CHESS

Everyman Publishers plc   www.everymanbooks.com

CONTENTS

BIBLIOGRAPHY

Books

The Sicilian Defence: Book One, Gligoric and Sokolov (Pergamon 1970)
The Ultimate Dragon: Volume 1, Gufeld and Stetsko (Batsford 2001)
The Ultimate Dragon: Volume 2, Gufeld and Stetsko (Batsford 2001)
The Sveshnikov Sicilian, McDonald (Batsford 1999)
The Complete Najdorf: Modern Lines, Nunn and Gallagher (Batsford 1998)
Beating the Sicilian 3, Nunn and Gallagher (Batsford 1995)
Winning with the Sicilian, Taimanov (Batsford 1991)
The Chess Struggle in Practice, Bronstein (Batsford 1980)
Secrets of Grandmaster Play, Nunn and Griffiths (Batsford 1987)
Encyclopaedia of Chess Openings 3rd Edition, (Sahovski Informator 1997)
Chess Informants 1-81

Internet

The Week In Chess 1-394
Chesspublishing.com

INTRODUCTION

One of the main problems facing many 1 e4 players is to find something to play against the Sicilian Defence. White's most interesting and aggressive lines are those based on 3 d4, yet the huge body of theory associated with the Open Sicilian makes the thought of playing this way quite daunting. The result is that players will often avoid the issue altogether by adopting relatively innocuous sidelines such as 2 c3 or lines with 3 ♗b5. Sometimes they will even switch to a different opening move. I have a theory that the surge in popularity of the Trompovsky (1 d4 ♘f6 2 ♗g5) is due to a large number of 1 e4 players looking for a sharp opening but with no Sicilian to worry about. I myself abandoned 1 e4 at an early stage of my career because I did not want to get involved in sharp Sicilian theory.

Grandmaster John Nunn attempted to help players solve this problem with his *Beating the Sicilian* and the subsequent revisions. For many these books were a godsend, yet the sharp lines that Nunn advocated have tended to date rather quickly. This meant that even once you finished the book there was an ongoing struggle to keep up with the theory. The other difficulty with Nunn's approach was that the lines he gave involved all sorts of different piece set-ups for White and at times quite intricate variations. Memorising such lines may not be difficult for someone with Dr.Nunn's remarkable abilities, but is certainly a problem for ordinary mortals who have limited time for chess study.

After having wrestled with these issues for a number of years, I could not help but notice that several strong grandmasters have found a solution that works well for them. By adopting the lines in which White fianchettoes his king's bishop they enjoy the space and attacking chances inherent in Open Sicilians, but manage to steer clear of the most highly analysed lines. The bishop on g2 protects White's e4-pawn, does not block the e-file and protects White's king should he castle kingside and then launch a kingside pawn storm.

The three main exponents of these lines are Grandmasters Petar Popovic, Sergei

Kudrin, and Alexander Ivanov, all of whom have enjoyed considerable success with them. There is also a host of international masters who play like this including Israel's Shimon Kagan and dozens of former Yugoslavs.

It struck me that the inherent economy of this approach made it very suitable for non-professionals, and thus the idea for this book was born. White plays Open Sicilians but reduces the need to memorise variations and understand typical positions by adopting the fianchetto lines. It is possible to adopt a set-up with g2-g3 against almost every form of Sicilian. In one or two cases White must vary his game plan but I have kept this to an absolute minimum.

In keeping with this principle of economy I have also only given what I think are the most suitable lines for White, and in some cases this is a blend of strength and the ease with which they can be learned. One other peculiarity that the reader will notice is that against 2 ♘f3 e6 I have given 3 ♘c3 followed by 4 d4 as my standard move order. This has no disadvantages for the suggested repertoire and avoids the complex and obscure Pin Variation with 3 d4 cxd4 4 ♘xd4 ♘f6 5 ♘c3 ♗b4; my aim throughout has been to avoid unnecessary complications.

The way I suggest you study this book is as follows:

1) **Familiarise** yourself with the basic patterns by playing through the games at speed. At this stage you should ignore the notes and sub-variations.

2) **Play** these lines in quick games at your local club or on the Internet (www.freechess.org or www.chessclub.com).

3) **Look up** the lines that occurred in your games and cross-check your play against the lines I recommend.

4) **Repeat** steps 2 and 3 for a month or two.

5) **Study** the book more carefully, working from cover to cover and making notes about any points of interest. Analyse the points of interest.

6) **Adopt** your new weapon in competitive games and matches.

7) **Analyse** your competitive games to establish what happened and whether either side could improve.

It remains for me to wish you every success in your forthcoming battles against the Sicilian. Any suggestions, comments or recommendations can be sent to me at ndavies@daviesplays.com.

Nigel Davies,
Southport,
November 2002

CHAPTER ONE

The Najdorf Variation

The Sicilian Najdorf has been in the theoretical limelight for the last 50 years. Popularised by the Argentinean Grandmaster Miguel Najdorf, it later became a firm favourite of two of the greatest ever World Champions, Bobby Fischer and Gary Kasparov. Throughout history White's attempts to refute the Najdorf have centred on 6 ♗g5 and 6 ♗c4, but Black has always found ways to defend himself. Whilst all this was going on, the 6 g3 variation has enjoyed a solid reputation but remained a relative backwater.

After 6 g3 Black has three main choices, the first of which is to transpose into the Classical Variation with 6...♘c6 (see Game 11 in Chapter 2). As 6...e6 leads into a Scheveningen Variation (Chapter 3), the only independent Najdorf line is with 6...e5. White in turn should answer this with 7 ♘de2 and not waste time trying to make 7 ♘b3 work.

Black meets 6 g3 by playing standard Najdorf ideas such as ...b7-b5, ...♗b7, ...♘c5 etc. The decision he must make concerns the order in which he plays

them. Against the standard plan in which Black plays ...b5-b4, exchanges knights on d5 and castles kingside, Spangenberg-Kasparov (Game 2) is a good model for White, not least because Spangenberg beats Kasparov rather easily. Kudrin seems to find an early push of his f-pawn quite irresistible in these positions, but it certainly worked out badly in Kudrin-Ftacnik (Game 1).

The danger of a white attack on the kingside has encouraged Black to delay castling; Kamsky-Gelfand (Game 3) sees Black attempt to improve his position on the queenside with 13...a5, whilst Black pushed the other rook's pawn with 13...h5 in Chiburdanidze-Zaichik (Game 4). From the available evidence these plans are fraught with danger for Black as his king is far from secure in the centre. The other problem Black faces is that ...b5-b4 allows White to take the initiative on the queenside with a2-a3.

Black has also tried to avoid these queenside issues by delaying ...b5-b4, instead re-routing his knight from d7 to c5 and (hopefully) e6. This was okay for Black in Kamsky-Wolff (Game 5), but Kindermann's 13 f4 (Game 6) looks much stronger, despite the unfortunate result of the game.

> ## Game 1
> ### Kudrin-Ftacnik
> Wijk aan Zee 1985

1 e4 c5 2 ♘f3 d6 3 d4 cxd4 4 ♘xd4 ♘f6 5 ♘c3 a6 6 g3 e5 7 ♘de2!

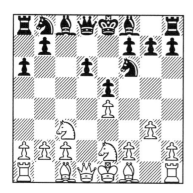

This is the most interesting and aggressive move, which intends to create an attacking kingside build-up with a later h2-h3, g3-g4 and ♘e2-g3.

7 ♘b3 is a much quieter line but this does not look very promising for White after 7...♘bd7 8 a4 b6 9 ♗g2 ♗b7 10 ♘d2 ♖c8 11 0-0 (Black's last move stops White from carrying out his plan of ♘d2-f1-e3, as after 11 ♘f1 ♖xc3 12 bxc3 ♘xe4 Black has excellent compensation for the exchange) 11...♗e7 12 ♖e1 ♖c5!? 13 ♘f1 ♕a8 14 ♘e3 (14 g4 ♖xc3 15 bxc3 ♘xe4 gave Black excellent play in Stoica-Stefanov, Rumanian Championship 1988) 14...♘xe4 15 ♘f5 ♘xc3 16 ♗xb7 ♕xb7 17 bxc3 g6 18

♘xe7 ♔xe7 19 ♗a3 ♖hc8!, which gave Black more than enough for the exchange in Popovic-King, Palma de Mallorca 1989.

7...b5!?

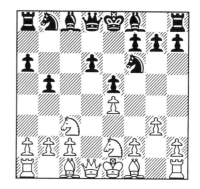

8 ♗g2

Black's last move is often delayed in favour of simple development, although White then has the option of preventing ...b5-b5 with 8 a4, which has been played by Karpov and Alexander Ivanov.

White can try to punish Black for playing ...b7-b5 so early with 8 a4 but then 8...♗b7 (8...b4 9 ♘d5 ♘xd5 10 ♕xd5 ♖a7 11 ♗e3 ♗e6 12 ♕d3 is uncomfortable for Black) 9 ♗g2 ♗e7 10 axb5 axb5 11 ♖xa8 ♗xa8 12 ♕d3 ♕a5 13 ♕xb5+ ♕xb5 14 ♘xb5 ♗xe4 was equal in the game Tompa-Schneider, Hungarian Championship 1977.

Another possibility is 8 ♗g5 but then 8...♘bd7 9 ♘d5 (9 a4 ♗b7 10 ♗g2 b4 11 ♘d5 a5 12 c3 ♗e7 13 ♗xf6 ♘xf6 14 ♘xf6+ ♗xf6 15 cxb4 axb4 16 ♕d2 was played in Kholmov-Zagrebelny, USSR 1988, and now Kholmov suggested 16...♗a6! 17 ♕xb4 ♖b8 18 ♕d2 ♗g5 with good compensation for the pawn) 9...♗e7 10 ♗xf6 ♘xf6 11 ♘ec3 ♗e6 12 a4 b4 13 ♘xb4 ♕a5 14 ♘c6 ♕c5 15 ♘xe7 ♔xe7 16 ♕d2 ♖hb8 and once again Black had good play for his pawn in Ivanov-De Firmian, USA Championship 1989.

It seems to me that if White has no way to take advantage of 7...b5, it is more economical to study the lines that just allow it. As we shall see, White gets good attacking chances.

8...♗b7

Usually 8...♘bd7 will transpose, but after 9 h3 Black can take the game down independent paths with 9...b4. Svidler-Har-Zvi, Duisburg 1992 continued 10 ♘d5 ♘xd5 11 exd5 a5 12 0-0 ♗a6 13 a3 ♗e7 14 ♗d2 ♕b6 15 axb4 axb4 16 ♗e3 ♕b5 17 ♘c1 0-0 and now 18 ♖e1 would have given White an edge.

9 0-0 ♗e7 10 h3

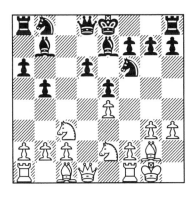

10...0-0

In a similar position Daniel King has proposed 10...h5!?, which restrains g3-g4 and asks where White's knight on e2 plans to go. On the other hand it is difficult to believe that this gratuitous weakening of Black's kingside can be good. Tests are needed to determine its merit.

11 g4 ♘bd7 12 ♘g3

The standard move, but not the only one. The significant alternative 12 g5 ♘e8 (12...♘h5 leaves Black with inadequate compensation for the pawn after 13 ♗f3 ♘f4 14 ♘xf4 exf4 15 ♗xf4 ♘e5 16 h4) 13 h4 ♘c7 (13...g6 14 ♘g3 ♘g7 is assessed by Ftacnik as unclear) 14 ♘g3 g6, intending 15...♘b6, is given as unclear by Ftacnik.

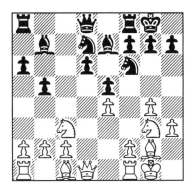

12...b4

For 12...♘c5 see Game 5. An interesting alternative is 12...g6, after which White should probably play 13 g5 ♘e8 14 h4 transposing into the previous note. After 13 ♗h6 Black can sacrifice the exchange with 13...♘c5!? 14 ♗xf8 ♗xf8 15 ♕d2 ♘e6 16 ♘ge2 h5 17 g5 b4 18 gxf6 bxc3 19 ♕xc3 ♖c8 20 ♕d2 ♕xf6, which gave him adequate compensation in Svidler-Hellers, Gausdal 1992.

13 ♘d5 ♘xd5

Black has also tried 13...♗xd5 14 exd5 ♘e8, but then 15 a3 bxa3 16 ♖xa3 ♗g5 17 ♗xg5 ♕xg5 18 ♕e2 ♘c7 19 c4 ♖ab8 20 ♘e4 ♕e7 21 ♕d2 ♘f6 22 ♘g3 ♖b6 23 ♘f5 ♕d8 24 b4 was clearly better for White in Kruszynski-Danner, Albena 1983.

14 exd5 g6

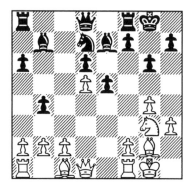

Black keeps the knight out of f5 but weakens the kingside. The alternative is to prepare a retreat square for the bishop on f8 with 14...♖e8 as in Game 2.

15 a3

At the time of the game this was a new move, but it is not necessarily better than the old one. Kindermann-Stohl, Trnava 1987 went 15 ♗h6 ♖e8 16 ♕d2! (hitting the b4-pawn like this is better than the immediate 16 f4?! which left White's king position weak after 16...♗f8 17 ♗xf8 ♖xf8 18 f5 ♖c8 19 ♔h2 ♖c5 20 ♕d2 ♕h4, Kudrin-Byrne, Berkeley 1984) 16...a5 17 f4 (17 a3 is also possible) 17...♗h4 18 ♘e4 ♘f6 19 ♘xf6+ ♗xf6 20 f5 with pressure on the f-file.

15...a5 16 ♗h6 ♖e8 17 f4?!

As in the game Kudrin-Byrne, White wastes no time in pushing his f-pawn forward. But once again it would have been better to play 17 ♕d2 with pressure against the b4-pawn.

17...♗a6 18 ♖f3 ♗h4 19 ♔h2

19 ♘e4 was probably better.

19...exf4 20 ♖xf4?

Underestimating the strength of Black's reply. 20 ♗xf4 was better, though White's king position still looks draughty after 20...♘e5 21 ♖e3 ♕b6.

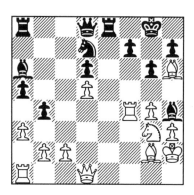

20...♗f6!

The transfer of the bishop to e5 gives Black a vitriolic attack. His bishop, knight and queen cooperate beautifully.

21 axb4 ♗e5! 22 ♖e4 ♕h4 23 ♗f4 ♘f6

Winning the exchange. Kudrin hopes to have some compensation with his queenside pawns, but a further mistake ends his resistance.

24 ♗xe5 ♘xe4 25 ♘xe4 ♖xe5

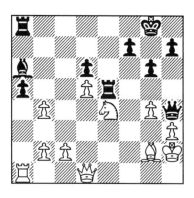

26 ♖xa5?

Allowing Black's attack to gain renewed vigour. White should play 26 ♕d4, which certainly gives him practical chances.

26...f5! 27 ♘g3

And not 27 ♘xd6 because of 27...♖e3!, threatening ...♕g3+.

27...f4 28 ♘h1

If 28 ♘e4 there follows 28...♖xe4 29 ♗xe4 ♕g3+ 30 ♔h1 ♕xh3+ 31 ♔g1 ♕e3+ etc.

28...♕e7 29 ♕d4 ♖e2 30 ♕xf4 ♖f8 31 ♕g3

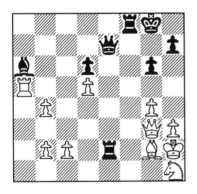

After 31 ♕d4 Black wins with 31...♖xg2+ 32 ♔xg2 ♕e2+ 33 ♘f2 ♕f3+ 34 ♔h2 ♗f1.

31...♖e3 32 ♖xa6 ♖xg3 33 ♘xg3 ♖f2 34 ♖c6 ♕e3 35 ♖c8+ ♔f7 36 ♖c7+ ♔e8 37 ♘h1 ♕f4+ 38 ♔g1 ♖d2 0-1

Game 2
Spangenberg-Kasparov
Buenos Aires (simultaneous) 1997

---

1 e4 c5 2 ♘f3 d6 3 d4 cxd4 4 ♘xd4 ♘f6 5 ♘c3 a6 6 g3 e5 7 ♘de2 ♗e7 8 ♗g2 b5 9 0-0 ♗b7 10 h3 ♘bd7 11 g4 b4 12 ♘d5 ♘xd5 13 exd5 0-0 14 ♘g3 ♖e8

For the time being Black avoids weakening his kingside, but White also has possibilities on the other flank.

14...g6 was featured in Game 1.

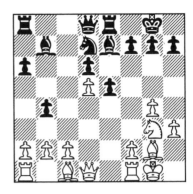

15 a3

Commencing queenside operations without further delay. It makes less sense to develop with 15 ♗e3 as if White later plays the thematic f2-f4 he will lose a tempo if he recaptures on f4 with his bishop.

15...a5

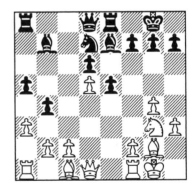

Black's main choice is to decide which of his queenside pawns will be weak. After 15...bxa3 16 ♖xa3 he is left with a weak a-pawn, the game Kindermann-Lutz, German Championship 1997 continuing 16...♘b6 17 ♖b3!? (17 b3 followed by 18 c4 seems more solid) 17...♗c8 18 f4 exf4 19 ♗xf4 ♗d7 20 ♖e1 ♖c8 21 ♘h5 with the better game for White.

16 ♗e3 ♗a6

As this was Kasparov's choice I will treat it as the main line, though Black has tried a couple of alternatives.

Occupying the c-file with 16...♕c7 is logical, but after 17 ♕d2 ♗a6 18 ♖fc1 ♖eb8 19 b3 ♘c5 20 axb4 ♖xb4 21 ♕e1 White threatened 22 ♗d2 and gave Black serious problems in Lima-Leitao, Sao Paulo 2001.

Black can exchange the dark-squared bishops with 16...♗g5 17 ♗xg5 ♕xg5 18 ♘e4 ♕h6 19 g5 ♕g6 20 h4 h5 as in Matulovic-Iashvili, Belgrade 1992, but then 21 ♘g3, hitting the h5-pawn, looks unpleasant for Black.

17 ♖e1 ♕b8 18 axb4 axb4 19 b3!

Fixing the weak pawn on b4.

19...♖c8 20 ♕d2 ♘c5 21 ♖a2!

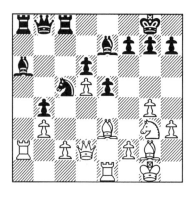

Turning the screw by doubling on the a-file. Black's position is already quite desperate.

21...♗b7 22 ♖ea1 ♖xa2 23 ♖xa2 ♗a8 24 ♘e4 ♘d7 25 ♖a4 ♕c7 26 ♖a7 ♕d8 27 ♘g3 ♗f8 28 ♕xb4 1-0

Although this game was played in a simultaneous display, this victory is a noteworthy achievement for the white player.

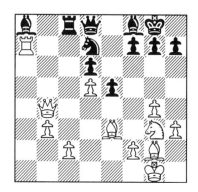

Game 3
Kamsky-Gelfand
Tilburg 1990

1 e4 c5 2 ♘f3 d6 3 d4 cxd4 4 ♘xd4 ♘f6 5 ♘c3 a6 6 g3 e5 7 ♘de2 ♗e7 8 ♗g2 b5 9 0-0 ♘bd7 10 h3 ♗b7 11 g4 b4

For 11...♘c5 12 ♘g3 0-0 see Game 5.

12 ♘d5 ♘xd5 13 exd5 a5

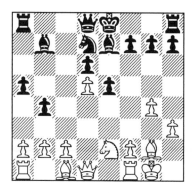

As this is almost always a useful move for Black, Gelfand decides to play it immediately. He also hopes that by delaying castling he will sidestep White's attempts to attack his king. For 13...h5 see the next game, while 13...0-0 transposes to previous games.

14 ♘g3 g6 15 ♗h6 ♗g5?

Gelfand probably wrongly assessed the position after White's 18th. He should settle for 15...♗a6, though this does look better for White after 16 ♖e1 ♗g5 17 ♗xg5 ♕xg5 18 ♘e4 ♕e7 19 f4 etc.

16 ♘e4! ♗xh6 17 ♘xd6+ ♔f8 18 ♘xb7 ♕b6

The knight on b7 is boxed in, but it cannot be taken and it supports the advance of White's c- and d-pawns.

19 d6 ♗f4

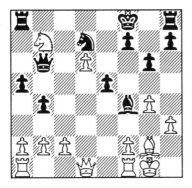

Black must defend the e-pawn before attacking the knight as 19...♖b8 20 ♕d5 ♘f6 is simply met by 21 ♕xe5. Kamsky pointed out that 19...♔g7 is refuted by 20 g5! ♗xg5 21 ♕g4, hitting both g5 and d7.

20 c4 ♖b8 21 ♕d5 ♘f6 22 ♕f3 g5?!

Black had to prevent White's next move by playing 22...♘d7.

23 c5 ♕a6 24 ♖fe1 h5

After 24...e4 there follows 25 ♖xe4 ♘xe4 26 ♕xe4 when White's passed pawns are unstoppable.

25 gxh5 ♖xh5 26 ♕e2 ♕a7 27 d7 e4 28 ♗xe4 ♖xh3

After 28...g4 Kamsky pointed out that White wins nicely with 29 ♗g6!

♕xb7 30 ♕e7+ ♔g7 31 ♕xf7+ ♔h6 32 ♗xh5 ♘xh5 33 ♖e6+ ♔g5 34 ♕g6+ ♔h4 35 ♕xg4 mate.

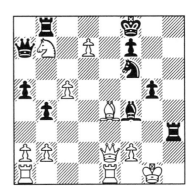

29 ♗g2 ♖h2 30 d8♕+ ♖xd8 31 ♕e7+ ♔g7 32 ♘xd8 1-0

Game 4
Chiburdanidze-Zaichik
Polanica Zdroj 1984

1 e4 c5 2 ♘f3 d6 3 d4 cxd4 4 ♘xd4 ♘f6 5 ♘c3 a6 6 g3 e5 7 ♘de2 ♘bd7 8 ♗g2 b5 9 0-0 ♗b7 10 h3 ♗e7 11 g4 b4 12 ♘d5 ♘xd5 13 exd5 h5!?

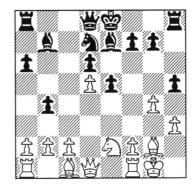

Attempting to weaken White's kingside like this looks quite interesting. The downside is that Black's position is not really geared towards kingside action and it does cost valuable time.

14 ♘g3

In Omeltschenko-Sanakoev, correspondence 1992 White tried another approach with 14 gxh5!? and after 14...♖xh5 15 ♘g3 ♖h7 16 a3 bxa3 17 ♖xa3 g6 18 f4 f5 19 fxe5 ♘xe5 20 ♘e2 ♗f6 21 ♖b3 ♕c8 the game was agreed drawn in a fascinating and double-edged position.

14...hxg4 15 hxg4 g6 16 a3 a5 17 ♕d2!?

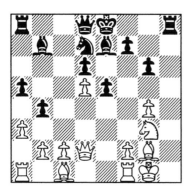

Attacking the b-pawn, but this has a highly artificial look about it even though it certainly forces Black's hand. 17 ♗e3 looks far more natural.

17...♗a6

Preparing to take the initiative rather than attempting passive defence. The lines 17...♖b8 18 axb4 axb4 19 ♖a4 and 17...bxa3 18 ♖xa3 both look very bad for Black.

18 ♖e1 b3 19 ♘e4

After 19 cxb3 ♘c5 Black threatens both b3 and d3.

19...bxc2 20 ♕xc2 ♖c8 21 ♕d1 ♖c4?!

Initiating a plan of counterattack which involves the sacrifice of the exchange, but in my view it looks down-

right bad. Black's king would be left horribly exposed after 21...f5 22 gxf5 gxf5 23 ♘g3 f4 24 ♘f5, with White threatening 25 ♗xf4 and 25 ♕g4 just for starters. The move 21...♘c5, however, looks reasonable.

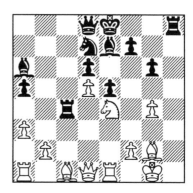

22 ♕f3 ♗c8 23 b3 ♖xe4

The logical follow-up because retreating the rook would leave Black very passive.

24 ♖xe4 ♘c5 25 ♖c4 f5 26 ♗b2 fxg4 27 ♖xg4?

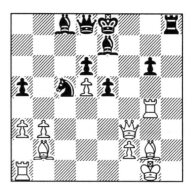

I don't understand this at all. After 27 ♕c3 White threatens both 28 b4 and 28 ♖xc5, the latter move returning the exchange for a massive attack.

27...♗xg4 28 ♕xg4 ♔f7 29 ♕f3+ ♔g7 30 ♖e1 ♖f8 31 ♕h3 ♗h4 32

♖e2 ♕f6 33 ♕e3 ♗g5

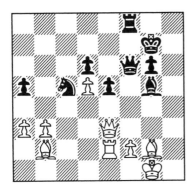

34 ♕xc5

With things not going to plan, White bails out into a drawn endgame.

34...dxc5 35 ♗xe5 ♖b8 36 ♗xf6+ ♗xf6 37 ♖e3 ♗d4 38 ♖d3 ♖f8 39 ♗f3 ♔f6 40 b4 axb4 41 axb4 ♔e5 42 bxc5 ♗xc5 ½-½

Game 5
Kamsky-Wolff
Long Beach 1993

---

1 e4 c5 2 ♘f3 d6 3 d4 cxd4 4 ♘xd4 ♘f6 5 ♘c3 a6 6 g3 e5 7 ♘de2 ♘bd7 8 ♗g2 b5 9 h3 ♗e7 10 g4 0-0 11 ♘g3 ♘c5

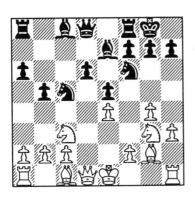

Aiming to come to e6 and probe the

f4-square.

12 0-0 ♗b7 13 ♗e3

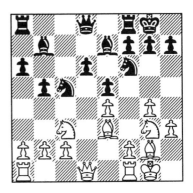

A sensible developing move, but 13 f4 may be better (see Game 6).

Defending against the possibility of ...b5-b4 with 13 a3 seems to be unnecessary but is doubtless quite playable. Ostojic-King, Dortmund 1987 continued 13...♖e8 14 ♗e3 g6 15 ♕d2 ♖c8 16 ♖ad1 ♘e6 17 ♖fe1 with equality.

13...♖c8 14 a3 g6 15 ♕d2 ♘fd7

In his notes Kamsky mentioned the possibility of 15...♘e6 and assessed the position arising after 16 ♘d5 ♘xd5 17 exd5 ♘f4 18 ♗xf4 exf4 19 ♘e2 ♗f6 20 c3 ♗e5 21 ♘d4 ♕f6 as unclear.

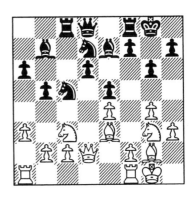

16 ♖ad1 ♘b6 17 b3 ♕c7 18 ♗h6 ♖fe8 19 ♘ge2 ♘e6

Threatening 20...♘d4 because of the unprotected position of the knight on c3. Kamsky's reply comes just in time.

20 ♘d5! ♘xd5 21 exd5 ♘f8 22 ♖c1 ♘d7?!

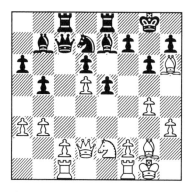

In playing this Black had overlooked something in his calculations. Better was 22...♕b8, though White still has the initiative after 23 f4 ♘d7 24 f5 etc.

23 c4 ♕b8

Black's original intention was probably 23...♘c5 24 cxb5 ♕d7, but then 25 bxa6 ♘xb3 26 axb7! ♖xc1 (26...♘xd2 27 bxc8♕ ♖xc8 28 ♗xd2 gives White more than enough for the queen) 27 ♕b4 ♖xf1+ 28 ♗xf1 ♖b8 29 ♕xb3 wins material.

24 ♔h1?

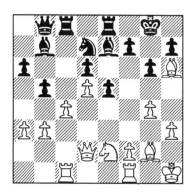

The wrong plan, which allows Black to build up strong pressure against the c4-pawn. White should play 24 cxb5 axb5 25 ♕a5, hitting the b5-pawn and putting Black in serious trouble.

24...bxc4 25 bxc4 ♖c7! 26 ♗e3 ♖ec8 27 ♕a2?!

And here 27 ♕b4 is a better try.

27...a5 28 ♖c2 ♗a6 29 ♖fc1 ♘c5?

Temporarily releasing the pressure on the c4-pawn, which gives White just enough time to free himself. The move 29...a4!, threatening 30...♕b3, was more precise.

30 ♖b1! ♖b7 31 ♖xb7 ♕xb7 32 ♘g3 ♕b3

After this White manages to hold the endgame. Instead, 32...♘b3 is met by 33 c5, and 32...♕d7 by 33 ♗xc5 ♖xc5 34 ♘e4 ♖c8 35 c5 etc.

33 ♕xb3 ♘xb3 34 ♗f1 a4

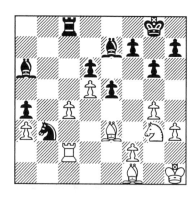

35 ♔g1!

And not 35 c5? ♗xf1 36 cxd6? because of 36...♖xc2 37 dxe7 ♗b5 stopping the pawn in its tracks.

35...♘a5 36 c5! ♗xf1 37 ♔xf1 dxc5 38 ♘e4 f5 39 d6 fxe4

39...♗f8? would have been a serious mistake because of 40 d7 ♖d8 41 ♗g5 ♖xd7 42 ♘f6+ etc.

40 dxe7 ♔f7?

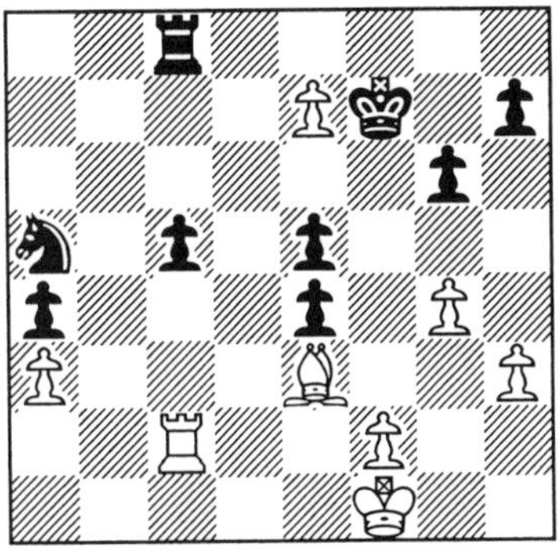

After this White draws easily. The last chance was to play 40...♘b3, when 41 ♖c4 ♔f7 42 ♖xa4 c4 makes the c-pawn very dangerous.

41 ♖xc5 ♖xc5 42 ♗xc5 ♘c6 43 e8♕+ ♔xe8 44 ♔e2 ♔d7 45 ♔e3 ♔e6 46 ♔xe4 ♘d8 47 h4 h5 48 gxh5 gxh5 49 f4 exf4 50 ♔xf4 ♘f7 51 ♗f8 ♘e5 52 ♔g5 ♘f3+ 53 ♔xh5 ♔d5 54 ♔g4

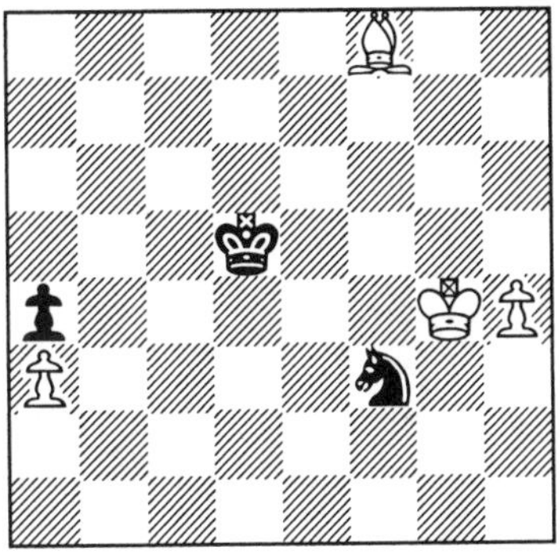

54...♘xh4 55 ♔xh4 ½-½

Game 6

Kindermann-Womacka

Bundesliga 1990

1 e4 c5 2 ♘f3 d6 3 d4 cxd4 4 ♘xd4 ♘f6 5 ♘c3 a6 6 g3 e5 7 ♘de2 ♘bd7 8 ♗g2 b5 9 h3 ♗b7 10 0-0 ♗e7 11 g4 ♘c5 12 ♘g3 0-0 13 f4!

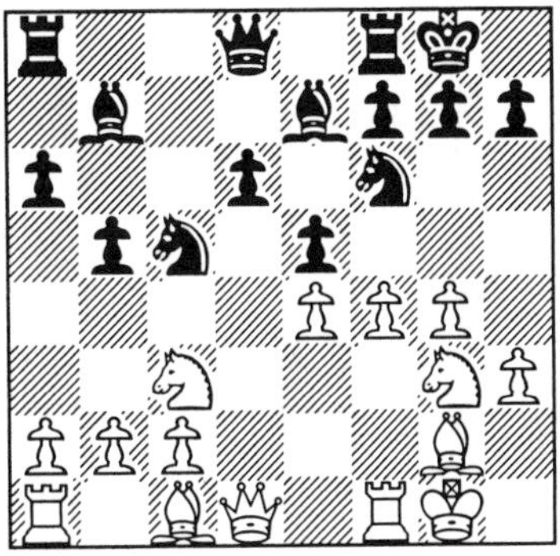

Notwithstanding the result of this game, this makes a lot of sense. White solves the problem of the f4-square immediately.

13...exf4

If Black doesn't capture White will push the pawn on to f5. After 13...b4 14 ♘d5 ♘xd5 15 exd5 ♗f6 there is 16 g5 ♗e7 17 ♘f5 with serious problems for Black.

14 ♗xf4

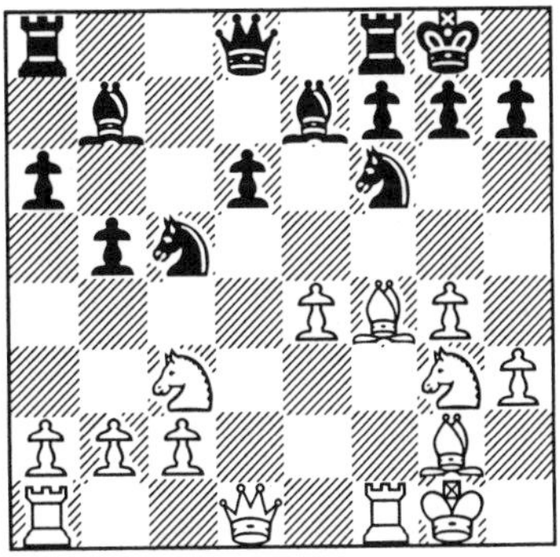

14...♘e6

If Black had played 14...b4 15 ♘d5 ♘xd5 16 exd5 ♗f6 he would have found himself in trouble after 17 ♘f5

♗xb2 18 ♗xd6 ♛b6 (18...♗xa1 19 ♛xa1 hits both c5 and g7) 19 ♔h1 ♗xa1 20 ♛xa1 f6 21 ♗xf8 ♖xf8 22 ♖e1.

White has a powerful passed d-pawn and better pieces.

15 ♗e3 ♘d7 16 ♘f5 ♘e5

Black's knight finds an outpost on e5, but after White's reply he must give up his light-squared bishop.

17 ♘d5 ♗xd5 18 exd5 ♘c7 19 b3 ♖e8 20 ♛d2 a5 21 ♘d4 ♛d7 22 ♘c6 ♗f6 23 g5 ♘xc6 24 gxf6

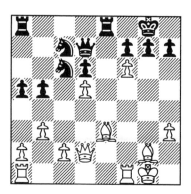

Playing for a direct attack. The endgame is also clearly better for White after 24 dxc6 ♛e7 25 gxf6 ♛xe3+ 26 ♛xe3 ♖xe3 27 ♖ad1 ♖d8 28 fxg7 but Kindermann wants more.

24...♘e5 25 ♗d4

There is a good case for playing 25 c3, after which 25...b4 26 c4 keeps the knight on c7 out of play.

25...b4 26 ♛g5 ♘g6 27 fxg7 ♘b5 28 ♗f6 ♖e2

Suddenly Black has annoying counterplay.

29 ♗f3 ♖xc2 30 ♗e4 ♛a7+ 31 ♔h1 ♖f2 32 ♛g3??

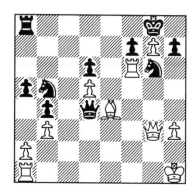

A truly horrific blunder that loses on the spot. Had White played 32 ♗g2, he would have retained dangerous threats after 32...♘c7 (or 32...♘c3 33 ♖xf2 ♛xf2 34 ♖f1) 33 ♖xf2 ♛xf2 34 ♖f1 ♛xa2 35 h4 etc.

32...♖xf6! 33 ♖xf6 ♛d4

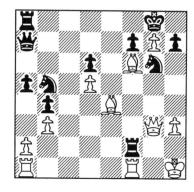

Suddenly attacking all of White's pieces.

34 ♖af1 ♕xe4+ 35 ♔h2 ♖a7 36 ♖e1 ♕xd5 37 ♖e8+ ♔xg7 38 ♖f2 ♖c7 39 ♕e3 ♖c3 40 ♕e1 ♘d4 0-1

Summary

After 6 g3 e5, the plan of 7 ♘de2 followed by an eventual h2-h3, g3-g4 and ♘e2-g3 sets some problems for Black which he has not yet really come to terms with. Certainly Black's position is playable, with the lines in which he delays ...b5-b4 looking more solid. But White has a definite space advantage and is frequently able to build a powerful attack.

CHAPTER TWO

The Classical Variation

The line 1 e4 c5 2 ♘f3 d6 3 d4 cxd4 4 ♘xd4 ♘f6 5 ♘c3 ♘c6 is one of the oldest forms of the Sicilian but it was not graced with a name until John Nunn chose to call it the Classical Variation. Black sensibly develops his knights and keeps his options open with regard to his pawns. After 6 g3 he can adopt either a Dragon set-up with 6...g6 or a Scheveningen with 6...e6, both of which transpose to the dedicated Scheveningen and Dragon chapters. Here we will examine lines of independent significance: 6...♗g4, 6...e5, 6...a6, 6...♕b6 and 6...♘xd4.

The move 6...♗g4 forces White to play 7 f3, after which his bishop will no longer be well placed on g2. White can, however, use the tempo gained with 7 f3 to switch plans and prepare a typical anti-Sicilian pawn storm with f2-f3 and g3-g4. This is particularly effective when Black's bishop retreats to d7. In a Scheveningen set-up it takes a possible retreat square away from Black's f6 knight (see Game 7), while in a Dragon it means that White can omit ♗f1-c4

because there's no danger of Black playing ...d6-d5 (see Game 8).

6...e5 is a plan pioneered by Isaac Boleslavsky. Black hopes that the space and central control offered by the pawn on e5 will offset the manageable weakness of the d5-square. Games 9 and 10 show Boleslavsky facing his own plan from the opposite side of the board, and in Game 9 he simply occupies d5 and then takes the initiative on the queenside after Black exchanges knights. This is familiar to us from Chapter 1.

With 6...a6 Black waits for White to commit his king's bishop with 7 ♗g2 before playing 7...♗g4. After this the move 8 f3 would be undesirable for White because it blocks his bishop in, but fortunately he has another plan with 8 ♘xc6 and 9 ♕d3 (see Game 11). Much has been written about how the exchange of knights on c6 strengthens Black's centre, but with the bishop on g2 the position resembles a kind of Grünfeld Defence with colours reversed. In Game 12 Black plays the rare but interesting 6...♕b6!? 7 ♘b3 ♗g4!? and reaches a very reasonable position out of the opening before losing a scrappy game.

Finally we come to Kaidanov-Yermolinsky (Game 13), in which Black attempts to transpose into a Dragon with 6...♘xd4 7 ♕xd4 g6. This sidesteps my suggested anti-Dragon plan of ♘de2 (see Chapter 6), but White can take the initiative with 8 e5!.

> ### Game 7
> ### Short-Tukmakov
> Hastings 1982/83

1 e4 c5 2 ♘f3 d6 3 d4 cxd4 4 ♘xd4 ♘f6 5 ♘c3 ♘c6 6 g3 ♗g4 7 f3 ♗d7

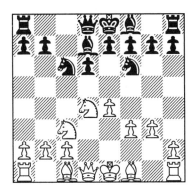

Black can also 'win' a pawn with 7...♘xd4 8 ♕xd4 ♗xf3 (8...♗d7 9 g4! is very awkward for Black) but White gets more than enough compensation with 9 ♗b5+ ♘d7 10 ♖f1! (10 0-0 ♗h5 11 ♕d5 ♕b6+ is an important defensive resource for Black). Now 10...♗h5 11 ♕d5 e5 12 ♕xb7 wins back the pawn with a clear advantage due to the control of d5 and the difficulty Black has with castling, while 10...♗g4 11 ♕d5 ♗e6 12 ♕xb7 ♕c8 (both 12...g6 and

12...a6 are strongly met by 13 ♘d5) 13 ♕xc8+ ♖xc8 14 ♗e3 ♖c7 15 ♘d5 ♗xd5 16 exd5 g6 17 ♗d4 f6 18 ♖f3 left White with a huge advantage in Faibisovich-Sleich, Decin 1996.

8 ♗e3 e6

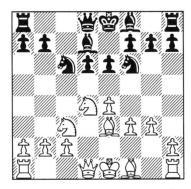

Deciding upon a 'Scheveningen' set-up in which Black places his pawns on d6 and e6. The problem with this particular one is that after a subsequent g3-g4-g5 by White, the knight on f6 lacks its natural retreat square on d7.

For the alternative 8...g6 see the next game.

9 ♕d2 a6 10 g4 b5

As this turns out badly, Black would do well to consider the alternatives:

a) 10...♗e7 11 0-0-0 (11 g5 ♘h5 leaves the g-pawn a bit vulnerable) 11...0-0 (11...♖c8 12 g5 ♘h5 13 ♘xc6 ♗xc6 14 ♗h3, intending ♗h3-g4, looks very awkward for Black) 12 h4 ♖c8 13 ♔b1 b5 14 h5 ♘xd4 15 ♗xd4 ♗c6 16 g5 ♘d7 17 g6 gave White a strong attack in Kiss-Csatari, Hungarian Women's Championship 1996.

b) 10...h6 11 h4 (11 0-0-0 is also possible) 11...♗e7 12 0-0-0 b5 13 ♗d3 ♕a5 14 ♔b1 ♘e5 15 g5 ♘h5 16 f4 was also good for White in Kudrin-Peters, Lone

Pine 1981.

c) 10...♞xd4 11 ♗xd4 ♗c6 12 g5 ♞d7 13 0-0-0 b5

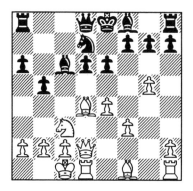

14 h4 b4 15 ♞e2 ♞e5 16 ♖h3 ♕a5 17 ♔b1 ♞c4 18 ♕e1 e5 19 ♗g1 ♗d7 20 ♖h2 ♗e6 21 ♞c1 ♗e7 22 f4 exf4 23 ♗xc4 ♗xc4 24 ♗d4 and White assumed the initiative in Kudrin-Goldin, Los Angeles 1991.

11 g5 ♞h5 12 0-0-0 ♖c8

Tukmakov later suggested 12...♞xd4 13 ♕xd4 ♗e7 14 f4 h6, though one wonders what the point is after 15 h4, and where Black's king intends to hide.

13 ♞xc6 ♖xc6 14 ♗h3!

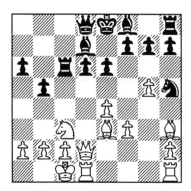

Simply threatening ♗h3-g4, which causes Black's knight on h5 considerable embarrassment.

14...h6

After 14...g6 there would follow 15 ♗g4 ♞g7 16 h4, when Black is very passive and faces the threat of h4-h5.

15 gxh6 gxh6

Perhaps 15...g6, at least trying to keep lines closed but leaving White's h6-pawn alive, offered more resistance.

16 ♖hg1 ♗g7 17 ♞e2 ♕e7 18 ♔b1!

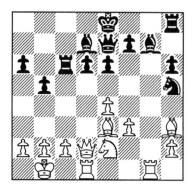

The winning move. White intends to bring his knight to b4 via c1 and d3, after which the pawns on a6 and d6 will be indefensible.

18...♔d8 19 ♞c1 ♔c8 20 ♞d3 ♖d8 21 ♕a5 ♔b7 22 ♞b4

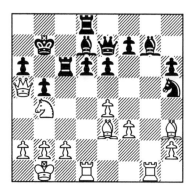

Winning the exchange for starters.

22...♖dc8 23 ♞xc6 ♖xc6 24 a4 ♕f6 25 ♗d4 ♕xd4 26 ♖xd4 ♗xd4 27

axb5 ⟨b6 28 bxa6+ ⟨a7 29 ⟨xh5 ⟨xb2+ 30 ⟨c1 ⟨a4 31 ⟨xf7+ ⟨xa6 32 ⟨f1+ ⟨b6 33 ⟨d3 1-0

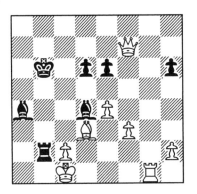

Game 8
Boleslavsky-Geller
Switzerland 1953

1 e4 c5 2 ⟨f3 ⟨c6 3 d4 cxd4 4 ⟨xd4 ⟨f6 5 ⟨c3 d6 6 g3 ⟨g4 7 f3 ⟨d7 8 ⟨e3 g6

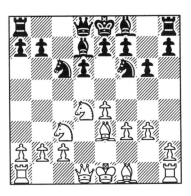

Opting for a Dragon formation which actually transposes into a line in which Black plays an early ...⟨d7. The disadvantage of this from Black's point of view is that he loses the possibility of playing ...d6-d5. This in turn means that White does not have to play ⟨f1-c4 in order to prevent this move.

9 ⟨d2 ⟨g7 10 0-0-0 0-0 11 g4

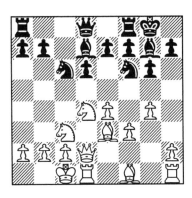

11...⟨c8

Black has also played 11...⟨e5 12 h4 and now:

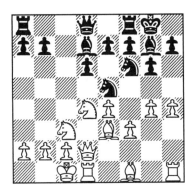

a) 12...⟨a5 13 ⟨b1 ⟨fc8 14 ⟨e2 ⟨c4 15 ⟨xc4 ⟨xc4 16 h5 ⟨ac8 17 ⟨b3 ⟨e5 18 ⟨d4 ⟨xd4 19 ⟨xd4 and Black had inadequate compensation for the exchange in Grischuk-Solovjov, Moscow 1999.

b) 12...b5 13 h5 b4 14 ⟨d5 ⟨xd5 15 exd5 ⟨a5 16 ⟨b1 ⟨xd5 17 hxg6 fxg6 18 ⟨h2 h6 19 ⟨e2! led to a strong attack in Bologan-Fedorov, Elista Olympiad 1998.

c) 12...h5 13 g5 (outright aggression with 13 ⟨e2!? hxg4 14 h5 gxf3 15 ⟨xf3 is very dangerous) 13...♘e8 14 f4 ♘g4 15 ♗g1 ♖c8 16 ♔b1 a6 17 ♖h3 b5 18 ♖d3 gave White strong central pressure in the game Bielczyk-Mikita, Slovakia 2001.

12 ♔b1

White can also consider the immediate 12 h4, after which 12...♘e5 13 h5 ♘c4 (or 13...♘xf3 14 ♘xf3 ♗xg4 15 h6! ♗h8 16 ♗e2 b5 17 a3 and Black has inadequate compensation for the piece according to Gufeld) 14 ♗xc4 ♖xc4 15 ♘b3 b5 16 hxg6 fxg6 17 e5! was strong in Kiselev-Golovchenko, St. Petersburg 2000.

12...♘e5 13 h4 b5

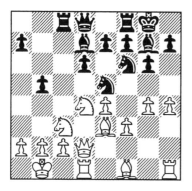

14 ♗h6

In view of the following exchange sacrifice, it might have been better to play 14 h5 as in Shabalov-Kiewra, St. Paul 2000. This game continued 14...b4 (if Black tries 14...♖e8 there could follow 15 hxg6 hxg6 16 ♗h6 ♗h8 17 ♗g5 with a strong attack) 15 ♘d5 e6 16 ♘xf6+ ♗xf6 17 g5 ♗h8 18 ♕xb4, when Black had inadequate compensation for the pawn.

14...♗xh6 15 ♕xh6 ♖xc3

With White threatening h4-h5, this is virtually forced.

16 bxc3 ♕a5 17 ♕e3 ♕a3

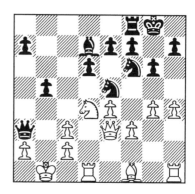

Black has nothing after 17...♘c4 18 ♗xc4 bxc4 19 ♔a1 ♖b8 20 ♖b1 etc.

18 h5 b4 19 ♕c1 ♕xc3 20 ♕b2 ♖c8

According to Bronstein, Black rejected 20...♕e3 because he did not want to accede to a draw by repetition after 21 ♕c1 (21 ♕b3!?) 21...♕c3 22 ♕b2 etc. But in the coming endgame he even stands worse.

21 hxg6 ♕xb2+

And not 21...hxg6 because of 22 ♕c1, intending ♕h6.

22 ♔xb2 hxg6

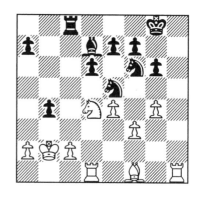

23 a3?!

An inaccuracy which was influenced by a complete oversight. White should prepare this move with either 23 ♗d3 or 23 ♗e2.

23...bxa3+ 24 ♚xa3??

Even now White can play 24 ♚a2 and avoid the worst.

24...♘xf3 25 ♘xf3 ♖c3+

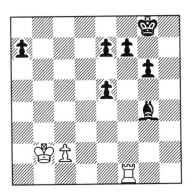

Apparently Boleslavsky had intended to block this check with 26 ♖d3! This miscalculation has left him with a hopeless endgame.

26 ♚b2 ♖xf3 27 e5 ♘xg4 28 ♗e2 ♖f2 29 ♗xg4 ♗xg4 30 ♖df1 ♖xf1 31 ♖xf1 dxe5

White's rook has no chance against the bishop and four pawns. Black now wins easily.

32 c4 ♚f8 33 ♖a1 ♗f3 34 c5 g5 35 ♖xa7 g4 36 ♖a3 ♚e8 37 ♚c1 f5 38 ♚d2 f4 39 ♖a6 g3 40 ♚e1 ♗e4 0-1

> *Game 9*
> ## Boleslavsky-Bondarevsky
> Garga 1953

1 e4 c5 2 ♘f3 ♘c6 3 d4 cxd4 4 ♘xd4 ♘f6 5 ♘c3 d6 6 g3 e5 7 ♘de2

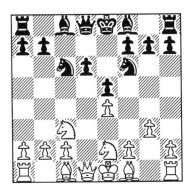

I prefer this retreat to 7 ♘b3, where the knight does not seem particularly well placed. Lamza-Rogers, Mendrisio 1988 continued 7...h6 8 ♗g2 ♗e7 9 0-0 0-0 10 h3 a6 11 a4 ♘b4 12 ♗e3 ♗e6 13 ♘d5 ♘bxd5 14 exd5 ♗f5 with a good game for Black.

The unusual 7 ♘f3 deserves a mention because it has been played by one of the gurus of the g3 lines, Petar Popovic. The game Popovic-Todorovic, Novi Sad 1992 continued 7...h6 8 ♗g2 ♗e7 9 0-0 0-0 10 ♖e1 ♖e8 11 h3 ♗f8 12 b3 a6 13 ♘d5 with slightly the better game for White.

7...♗e7

Black has also tried an interesting pawn sacrifice with 7...d5!?. Now 8 ♘xd5 ♗g4 9 ♕d3 ♘xd5 is very unpleasant for White, but 8 exd5 ♘b4 9 a3 ♘bxd5 10 ♘xd5 ♘xd5 11 ♗g2 ♗e6 12 0-0 (12 b3!?, intending c2-c4, is also worth considering) 12...♕d7 13 c4 ♘b6 14 ♕xd7+ ♘xd7 15 ♗xb7 ♖b8 16 ♗c6 ♗xc4 17 ♖d1 ♗b5 18 ♗xb5 ♖xb5 19 b4 left White better because of his queenside pawn majority in Mestel-Kinsman, Lloyds Bank Masters, London 1985.

For the attempt to exploit the weakness of f3 with 7...♗g4 see the next game.

8 ♗g2

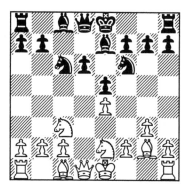

8...0-0

Black has also tried an early advance of his h-pawn, but Kudrin-Van der Wiel, Wijk aan Zee 1985 left Black's kingside looking vulnerable after 8...h5 9 h3 h4 10 g4 ♘h7 11 ♘d5 ♗g5 12 f4 exf4 13 ♘exf4 0-0 14 0-0 ♘e5 15 a4.

In Stanke-Baklan, Hamburg 1999 Black tried 8...a6 9 ♗g5 and only then 9...h5, but this should be better for White after just 10 0-0 (in the game he played 10 ♕d2 which looks somewhat artificial) 10...♗e6 11 ♗xf6 ♗xf6 12 ♘d5 etc.

In Dzindzichashvili-McLaughlin, USA 1990 Black played 8...♗e6 9 h3 ♕d7?! but this gave White a good game after 10 ♘d5 ♗xd5 11 exd5 ♘b4 12 0-0 ♖c8 13 c3 ♘a6 14 ♗e3 b5?! 15 b4, intending 16 a4.

9 0-0 a6

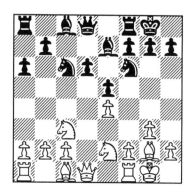

Another move worth considering for Black is 9...♗e6, for example 10 ♘d5 ♗xd5 (10...♘d7 is possible, though White must be better) 11 exd5 ♘b8 (11...♘a5 12 b3 left Black's knight very badly offside in Bogoljubov-Heinicke, Nuremberg 1949) 12 c4 ♘fd7! (this is better than 12...♘bd7 as Black can now try to hold the queenside by putting his other knight on a6 and he introduces the possibility of exchanging his dark-squared bishop) 13 ♗e3 a5 14 ♖b1 ♘a6 15 ♕d2 ♖c8 16 b3 g6 17 ♘c3 was agreed drawn in Marinkovic-Kosten, Belgrade 1988, though my own preference would be for White.

In Kudrin-Piket, Brussels 1987 Black tried not to commit himself too heavily by playing 9...h6 10 h3 ♖e8 11 ♗e3 ♗f8, when a complex and intricate struggle developed after 12 ♕d2 ♗e6 13 g4!? (13 ♖fd1 ♕d7 14 ♔h2 is a more circumspect way to play the position) 13...♕d7 14 ♘g3 ♖ac8 15 ♖fd1 b6 16 b3 ♘e7 17 a4 ♘g6 18 ♘b5 etc.

10 h3

After 10 a4 Black can cover the d5-square with 10...♘b4.

10...b5 11 ♗e3 b4

White can meet 11...♘a5 with 12 b3 ♕c7 13 ♕d2 ♗b7 14 g4!? (14 a4 b4 15 ♘d5 ♗xd5 16 exd5 ♖ab8 17 f4 exf4 18 ♖xf4 ♘h5 19 ♖f2, as in Inkiov-Spassov, Pernik 1981, is another interesting way to play it) 14...♖ac8 15 ♖ac1 ♖fd8 16 ♘d5 ♗xd5 17 exd5 ♘d7 18 ♘g3 and White stood better in the game Keller-Gromek, Moscow 1956.

In the game Kudrin-Kosten, Geneva 1988 Black led the game along the paths of the Sicilian Najdorf with 11...♗b7 12 ♕d2 ♘b8!?, though the loss of time involved with this manoeuvre led to difficulties for Black after 13 g4 ♘bd7 14 ♘g3 b4 15 ♘d5 ♘xd5 16 exd5 a5 17 a3, with White having pressure on both sides of the board.

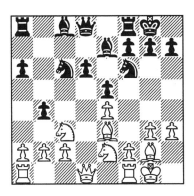

12 ♘d5 ♘xd5 13 exd5 ♘a5

In Chistiakov-Geller, USSR 1955 White obtained pressure along the same lines as the game after 13...♘b8 14 a3 bxa3 15 ♖xa3 ♘d7 16 ♕d2 ♖b8 17 b3 f5 18 f4, when Black's kingside hopes have come to nothing and he is left facing serious pressure on the other flank.

14 b3 ♘b7

With the knight having been denied the c4-square, it's time to try repositioning the beast. But even on b7 it does

not have a great future.

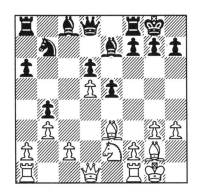

15 ♕d2 a5 16 a3 bxa3 17 ♖xa3 ♗d7 18 f4 ♖c8

It must have been a difficult decision for Black to allow the pawn to advance to f5, but 18...exf4 19 ♗xf4 gives White's knight access to d4 and c6.

19 f5 a4 20 b4 ♖c4 21 g4 h6 22 ♘g3 ♗g5 23 ♗xg5 ♕xg5 24 ♕xg5 hxg5 25 c3

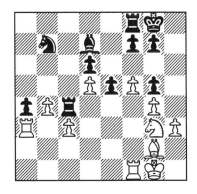

Effectively deciding the game. None of Black's pieces can really do anything, with the knight on b7 being particularly ineffective. Meanwhile White can bring his pieces round to pick off Black's weak pawns.

25...f6 26 ♘e4 g6 27 fxg6 ♔g7 28 ♘d2 ♖c7 29 ♗e4 ♗e8 30 c4 ♘d8

31 ♖c1 ♗xg6 32 ♗xg6 ♔xg6 33 ♖xa4

The first casualty. And with White's queenside ready to roll the end is nigh.

33...♘f7 34 b5 ♖h8 35 ♔g2 f5 36 gxf5+ ♔xf5 37 b6 ♖b7 38 ♖a7 ♘d8 39 ♖f1+ ♔g6 40 ♖xb7 ♘xb7 41 ♘e4 1-0

Game 10
Boleslavsky-Shagalovich
USSR 1955

---

1 e4 c5 2 ♘f3 ♘c6 3 d4 cxd4 4 ♘xd4 ♘f6 5 ♘c3 d6 6 g3 e5 7 ♘de2 ♗g4

A sharp attempt to exploit the f3-square, which does not meet with noticeable success.

8 ♗g2 ♘d4

Black has also tried 8...♕d7 but then 9 h3 ♗e6 10 ♘d5 ♗e7 11 ♗e3 left Black struggling to get counterplay in Grigorov-Sirigos, Peristeri 1992. The big problem with Black putting his bishop on e6 is that after White brings his knight to d5 it can only be exchanged off with Black's light-squared bishop.

9 0-0! ♖c8

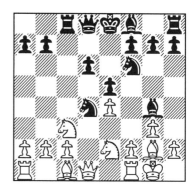

White's nonchalant last move leaves Black struggling. 9...♘f3+ 10 ♔h1 h5 is simply met by 11 ♕d3.

10 h3 ♗xe2?!

Trying to win a pawn. A sounder way to play it is with 10...♘xe2+ 11 ♘xe2 ♗e6, though White's position was still preferable after 12 ♘c3 ♗e7 13 ♗e3 0-0 14 ♕d2, intending a2-a4 and ♖fd1.

11 ♘xe2 ♘xc2 12 ♖b1 ♗e7

After 12...♘b4 White can play 13 ♕b3, when the attempt to keep the b7-pawn with 13...♕b6 is strongly answered by 14 ♗e3 ♕b5 15 ♘c3 etc.

13 ♗d2 0-0 14 ♗c3 b5 15 ♖c1 ♘d4?!

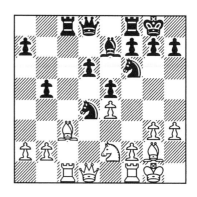

A better chance to stay in the game was with 15...b4, after which 16 ♗d2

♕c7 17 ♗xb4 ♕b6! 18 ♗c3 ♘b4 19 ♖a1 ♖c7 gives Black a bit of counter-play to offset his clear strategic inferior-ity. After the text he has nothing.

16 ♘xd4 exd4 17 ♕xd4 ♕d7 18 ♗b4 ♕e6?!

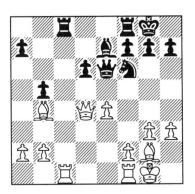

A rather desperate-looking move which does not help matters.

19 ♖xc8 ♖xc8 20 ♕xa7 h5 21 e5!
♘e8 22 ♕b7 ♗f8 23 ♗d5 ♕f5 24 e6
1-0

Game 11
Pilnik-Sanguinetti
Mar del Plata 1954

---

1 e4 c5 2 ♘f3 d6 3 d4 cxd4 4 ♘xd4 ♘f6 5 ♘c3 a6

Whilst this particular game features the Najdorf order of moves, a more common way of reaching this line is via 5...♘c6 6 g3 a6. Black's idea is to play a useful waiting move with ...a7-a6 before flicking in ...♗c8-g4.

6 g3 ♘c6 7 ♗g2 ♗g4 8 ♘xc6!

If White plays 8 f3 in this position, the bishop on g2 is poorly placed. The game Hübner-Short, Garmisch-Parten-kirchen 1994 continued 8...♗d7 9 ♗e3 e6 10 g4 h6 11 ♘xc6 ♗xc6 12 ♕d2 d5

with approximate equality.

8...bxc6 9 ♕d3 ♕c8

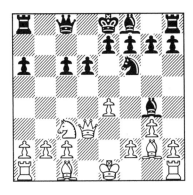

Preparing to exchange the light-square bishops with 10...♗h3. When White prevents this with his next move he can not easily castle kingside. After other moves White has also preferred a kingside pawn advance, though he also has an effective and less risky plan available.

a) 9...♗d7 was played in Gligoric-Stahlberg, Amsterdam 1950, and after 10 h3 e5 11 0-0 h6 I like the idea of playing 12 b3 followed by either ♗c1-a3 or ♗c1-b2, ♘c3-a4 and c2-c4 with the positional threat of c4-c5. In the game White played 12 ♗e3 ♗e7 13 ♖ad1 0-0 14 f4 which led to a complex and full-blooded struggle after 14...exf4 15 gxf4 ♕a5.

b) 9...e5 10 h3 (10 f4 ♗d7 11 h3 ♗e7 12 g4 0-0 13 f5 d5 14 0-0 d4 led to a sharp game in Reshevsky-Najdorf, Am-sterdam 1950) 10...♗d7 11 0-0 h6 (after 11...♗e7 White can make life unpleasant with 12 ♗g5, threatening to capture on f6) 12 b3 ♗e7 13 ♗b2, intending ♘c3-a4 and c2-c4 yet again.

10 h3 ♗e6?!

To me this looks dubious as the

bishop is not well placed here and Black is unable to move his e-pawn. 10...♗d7 looks like a better try.

11 f4

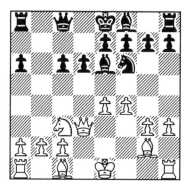

I prefer the direct approach in this position to those in which Black has played ...e7-e5 already. But White still has a quieter option available in 11 b3, for example 11...g6 12 ♗b2 ♗g7 13 ♘a4 ♕b7 14 e5! and White retains some advantage.

11...g6 12 g4 ♘d7 13 b3 ♗g7 14 ♗b2 a5 15 ♘d1 ♘c5 16 ♕e3 ♗xb2 17 ♘xb2 f6

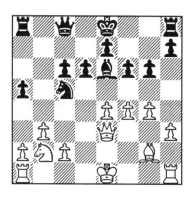

Making room for his bishop on f7 so that after White plays f4-f5, Black's knight can come to e5 via f7.

18 e5 ♔f7?!

Black's king is not at all safe on this square. Black should simply play 18...0-0 with a playable game.

19 0-0 a4?

And after this Black falls victim to a beautiful combinative breakthrough. He should blockade the kingside with 19...f5.

20 ♖ad1 ♖d8 21 f5!!

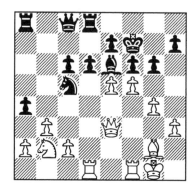

Breaking open the position and making room for his queen to go to h6.

21...gxf5 22 exd6 exd6 23 ♕h6! ♔g8 24 ♕xf6

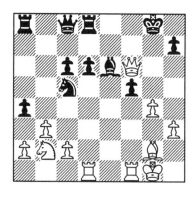

24...♖a7

Here Black might have overlooked White's 29th. After 24...fxg4 there follows 25 ♖xd6 ♖xd6 26 ♕g5+ ♔h8 27 ♕e5+ ♔g8 28 ♕xd6 gxh3 29 ♗xc6 ♖a6

30 ♕g3+ with a huge advantage.

25 gxf5 ♖f7 26 ♕h6 ♖xf5 27 ♖xf5 ♗xf5 28 ♕g5+ ♗g6

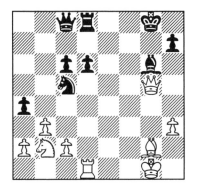

29 ♗xc6!

Not only winning a pawn, but also securing the huge d5-square for his bishop. Thus far everything has gone beautifully for White, but with the time control approaching the game descends into chaos.

29...axb3 30 ♗d5+ ♔g7 31 ♖f1 ♘d7 32 axb3

32 cxb3 is better, removing the c-pawn from its vulnerable current location.

32...♖e8 33 ♘d3

And here 33 ♘c4 looks stronger.

33...♔h8 34 ♕g2?

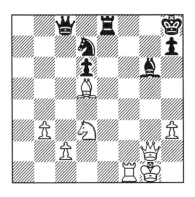

Overlooking Black's stunning reply. 34 ♖f2 would still leave White with a winning position.

34...♗e4! 35 ♗xe4 ♖g8

Winning the queen. Fortunately for White he can construct a blockade.

36 ♕xg8+ ♔xg8 37 ♖f2 ♘b6 38 ♗f5 ♕e8 39 ♖g2+ ♔h8 40 ♖f2 ♕e3 41 ♔g2 ♘d5 42 ♗g4 ½-½

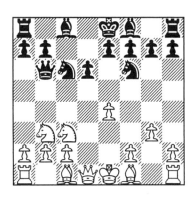

Game 12
Short-Murey
Brighton 1983

---

1 e4 c5 2 ♘f3 d6 3 d4 cxd4 4 ♘xd4 ♘f6 5 ♘c3 ♘c6 6 g3 ♕b6 7 ♘b3

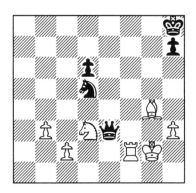

Far and away White's most natural move, 7 ♘b3 covers the b2-pawn and prepares to gain time on Black's queen with a later ♗e3.

Some strong players have played 7 ♘f3, though it is difficult to imagine that this can harm Black if he defends accurately. Popovic-Deze, Novi Sad 1981 continued 7...e6 8 ♗g2 ♗e7 9 0-0 0-0 10 ♘d2 ♘e5 11 ♕e2 ♗d7 12 ♔h1 ♗c6 (12...♖fc8 13 f4 ♘g6 looks playable) 13 f4 ♘ed7 14 ♘b3 e5?! (14...♖fd8 looks more flexible) 15 f5 with a clear edge for White, though as noted Black could improve his chances at several different points.

The speculative 7 ♗e3 looks unsound after 7...♕xb2 8 ♘db5 ♗g4 9 ♖b1 ♕xc3+ 10 ♘xc3 ♗xd1 11 ♔xd1 0-0-0 12 ♗b5 ♘g4, when White had inadequate compensation in Kiss-V.Zaitsev, Budapest 1996.

7...♗g4

Continuing to play in enterprising style. Black can also lead the game along lines typical of the Scheveningen Variation by playing 7...e6, though White gains time compared with a classic 6 ♗e2 Scheveningen because his bishop is on g2 already (rather than having to go from e2-f3-g2): 8 ♗g2 ♗e7 9 0-0 0-0 10 ♗e3 ♕c7 11 f4 a6 12 a4 b6 (12...♘a5 13 ♘xa5 ♕xa5 14 ♕d2 ♕c7 15 a5 left Black passive in Am.Rodriguez-Corral Blanco, Barcelona 2000) 13 g4 ♖e8 14 g5 ♘d7 15 ♖f3 ♗f8 16 ♖h3 g6 17 ♕e1 ♗b7 18 ♕f2 ♗g7 19 ♖f1 ♘b4 20 f5! (the storm breaks) 20...exf5 21 exf5 ♗xg2 22 ♔xg2 ♕c4 (22...♘f8 23 f6 ♗h8 shut Black's dark-squared bishop out of the game in Damjanovic-Cabrilo, Yugoslav Team Championship 1996) 23 ♖h4 ♕c6+ 24 ♔g1 ♘xc2 25 fxg6 f5 26 ♕xf5 ♕g2+ 27 ♔xg2 ♘xe3+ 28 ♔g1 ♘xf5 29

gxh7+ ♔h8 30 ♖xf5 and White went on to win the endgame in Popovic-Damjanovic, Yugoslav Team Championship 1996.

In Kuzmin-Kremenietsky, Moscow 1984 Black played the unusual 7...♗e6 but after 8 ♗e3 ♕c7 9 ♘d5 ♗xd5 10 exd5 ♘e5 11 ♗g2 g6 12 0-0 ♗g7 13 ♗d4 0-0 14 a4 ♖fe8 15 ♘d2 White had a nice advantage in space.

8 ♗e2!?

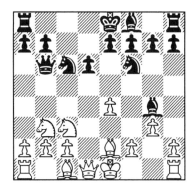

Aiming for quick development like this seems to be White's most promising option. White has also played 8 f3 but this offers him nothing after 8...♗e6 and now:

a) 9 ♘d5 gives Black good counterplay after 9...♗xd5 10 exd5 ♘b4 11 c4 g6 12 a3 ♘a6 13 ♕d3 ♗g7 due to the pressure exerted on the dark squares by Black's queen and bishop, Marinkovic-Popovic, Niksic 1997.

b) 9 ♕e2 ♘b4 10 ♗g5 (10 ♗e3? ♕xe3 11 ♕xe3 ♘xc2+) 10...a6 (10...♖c8 11 ♕b5+ ♘d7 12 ♕xb6 ♘xb6 13 ♗b5+ ♗d7 14 ♗xd7+ ♘xd7 15 0-0-0 was slightly better for White – though shortly agreed drawn – in Milosevic-Groszpeter, European Club Cup, Thessaloniki 1996) 11 0-0-0 ½-½ Popovic-

Groszpeter, Vienna 1996.

8...♗xe2 9 ♕xe2 e6 10 ♗e3 ♕c7 11 0-0-0 a6 12 g4 g6?!

The development of Black's bishop on g7 leaves the central dark squares vulnerable. Black should play 12...♗e7 13 g5 ♘d7 with a double-edge game in prospect.

13 g5 ♘d7 14 f4 0-0-0 15 ♕f2 ♗g7?

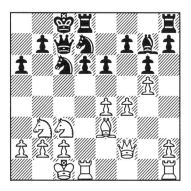

Continuing with his plan, which leads to serious difficulties for Black. The solid alternative 15...♔b8 16 ♘a4 ♖c8 followed by ...♗f8-e7 was indicated here.

16 ♘a4 b5?

A nervous-looking move that allows White to take the initiative. Black should try to batten down the hatches with 16...♔b8 17 ♘b6 ♖he8 followed by ...♗g7-f8.

17 ♘b6+ ♔b7 18 e5! ♗f8

After 18...♘xb6 there follows 19 exd6 ♖xd6 (19...♗xb2+ is met by 20 ♔b1, when Black is left with a lot of hanging pieces) 20 ♖xd6 ♕xd6 21 ♗xb6, when Black's king looks very exposed.

19 exd6 ♗xd6 20 ♖xd6 ♕xd6 21 ♖d1??

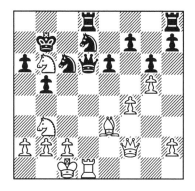

In playing this way White either overlooked Black's reply or wrongly assessed the resulting position. He should play 21 ♘xd7 ♖xd7 22 ♘c5+ ♔c7 23 ♘xd7 ♕xd7 24 ♖d1, when White's position is preferable because of his safer king.

21...♕xd1+ 22 ♔xd1 ♘xb6+ 23 ♔c1 ♘a4

Covering the c5-square and preparing to double his rooks on the d-file.

24 c3 ♖d5 25 ♔c2 ♖c8

A stronger way to play would have been 25...h6 26 gxh6 ♖xh6, which brings the other rook into play. The following plan of a queenside pawn advance seems to me to be rather misguided.

26 a3 a5 27 ♘d2 ♘e7 28 ♘e4 ♘f5 29 ♘f6 ♖d6 30 ♕f3+ ♔a6 31 ♗f2 ♘b6 32 ♕h3 ♘d4+

Flashy but ineffective. Black should aim to exchange off his number one enemy, the knight on f6. The line 32...♘d5 33 ♘xd5 (33 ♕xh7 ♘xf6 34 gxf6 ♖d7 holds everything and leaves White to face the music) 33...♖xd5 34 ♕xh7 ♖cd8 35 ♔b3 ♖d2 is strong for Black.

33 ♗xd4 ♖xd4 34 ♕xh7 ♖xf4 35

♕xf7 ♖h8 36 ♕xe6 ♖xh2+ 37 ♔d3
♖f3+ 38 ♔d4

White's king treads carefully through the minefield. 38 ♔e4?? loses the queen to 38...♖e2+.

38...♖d2+??

The decisive mistake, which carelessly drives White's king into an attacking position. 38...♖f5 was the right move.

39 ♔c5 ♖f5+ 40 ♔c6 ♖d8 41 ♘e8 ♖c8+ 42 ♘c7+ ♖xc7+ 43 ♔xc7 ♖c5+ 44 ♔d6 ♖xg5 45 ♔c6 ♖d5 46 ♕e7 ♖d7 47 ♕c5 1-0

Game 13
Kaidanov-Yermolinsky
US Championship, Parsippany 1996

---

1 e4 c5 2 ♘f3 d6 3 d4 cxd4 4 ♘xd4 ♘f6 5 ♘c3 ♘c6 6 g3 ♘xd4 7 ♕xd4 g6 8 e5!

A powerful idea that casts doubt upon the accuracy of Black's move order. If White plays 8 ♗g2 then after 8...♗g7 9 0-0 0-0 we reach a normal g3 Dragon, but one in which Black has exchanged a pair of knights and White does not have the opportunity of retreating with ♘de2.

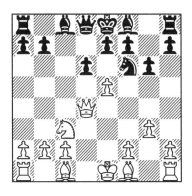

8...dxe5 9 ♕xe5 ♗g7 10 ♗g2

The attempt to catch Black's king in the middle with 10 ♗b5+ ♗d7 11 ♗g5 (11 0-0 ♗xb5 12 ♕xb5+ ♕d7 is nothing for White) can be nonchalantly ignored with 11...0-0 12 0-0-0 ♕a5!, when Yermolinsky's analysis continues 13 ♕xe7 ♗xb5 14 ♗xf6 ♖fe8 15 ♕d6 ♖e6 16 ♕d5 ♗xf6 17 ♘xb5 ♖e5 18 ♕xb7 ♖xb5 19 ♕xa8+ ♔g7 with a winning attack.

10...0-0 11 0-0 ♗f5

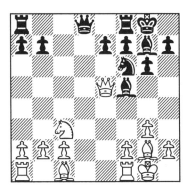

After 11...♗e6 White has a strong move in 12 ♕b5!.

12 ♕e2

At the time of the game this was a new move. One can only assume that 'Yermo' had an improvement in mind against the older 12 ♕b5, though current theory still respects a couple of wins by Petar Popovic. The game Popovic-Piket, Lucerne 1989 went 12...♗xc2 13 ♕xb7 ♖b8 (13...♕a5 14 ♗f4 ♖ac8 15 ♕xe7 ♖fd8 16 ♖ac1 left Black a pawn down for nothing in Popovic-Wilder, Dortmund 1988) 14 ♕xa7 e6 15 h3 ♕c8 16 a4, with Black being left in desperate trouble.

12...e6! 13 ♗xb7 ♖b8 14 ♗f3 h5 15 ♖b1 ♘g4!

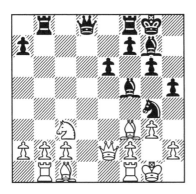

Going for active counterplay to compensate for the lost pawn. After 15...♘d5 there is 16 ♘xd5 exd5 17 ♗f4, when 17...♖xb2 18 ♖xb2 ♗xb2 19 c4 obtains an extra passed d-pawn.

16 ♘e4

Another possibility was 16 ♗f4, after which 16...e5 17 ♗e3 ♘xe3 18 fxe3 leaves White a pawn up in a position which is admittedly difficult to win.

16...♘e5 17 ♗g2 ♗g4 18 f3

After 18 ♕e3 Black gets good compensation with 18...♕c7 19 c3 ♘c4. A draw by repetition might result after 20 ♕f4 e5 21 ♘f6+ ♔h8 22 ♕g5 ♗f5 23 ♗e4 ♗xe4 24 ♘xe4 ♘a3 etc.

18...♗f5 19 ♖d1 ♕a5 20 a3 ♖fc8 21 ♗f4 ♗xe4?

A mistake which throws away some

of Black's compensation. He should have played a preliminary 21...♕a4. Then 22 c3 ♗xe4 23 fxe4 (23 ♕xe4 ♕xe4 24 fxe4 ♖b3 will win the b2-pawn with the better game) 23...♖d8 gives Black good compensation for his pawn because of his invulnerable knight on e5, White's bad bishop on g2 and the weakness of White's king.

22 ♕xe4 ♕c5+?

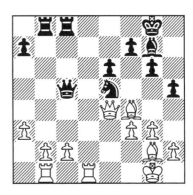

And here 22...♖c4 was a better try.

23 ♔h1 ♖d8

Not 23...♕xc2?? because of 24 ♖d8+ winning a rook.

24 ♖e1 ♖d5

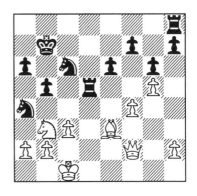

25 ♕e2

25 c4! ♘d3 26 ♗e3 was a much crisper way to play the position.

25...♖bd8 26 ♗e3 ♕c4 27 b3 ♕xe2 28 ♖xe2 a5 29 f4?

A time-trouble error which lets Black back into the game. White should first play 29 ♔g1, when the win is not in doubt.

29...♖d1+ 30 ♖e1 ♖xe1+ 31 ♖xe1 ♘g4 32 ♗b6 ♖d2 33 h3 ♘h6 34 ♗e4 ♘f5 35 ♗xf5 gxf5 36 c4?

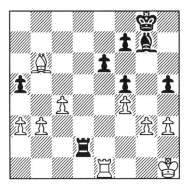

According to Kaidanov, White should play 36 ♗xa5 ♖xc2 37 ♗b6 ♖c3 38 ♖e3, which wins easily enough. Now Black is able to hold a draw.

36...♖b2! 37 ♖e3 a4 38 b4 ♖b3 39 b5 ♔f8 40 ♔g2 ♔e8?

The final error. Black could have held a draw with 40...♗b2 41 ♗c5+ ♔e8 42 ♔f2 ♗c1 43 ♖f3 ♖b2+ 44 ♔e1 ♖c2 45 b6 ♔d7 46 ♖d3+ ♔c8 etc.

41 ♔f3 ♗f8 42 ♔e2 ♖xa3 43 ♖xa3 ♗xa3 44 ♗d4 ♔d7 45 c5 f6 46 c6+ ♔c7 47 ♗xf6 1-0

Summary

Whilst there are a number of ways for Black to play this line, there is nothing which looks very comfortable. His most solid options are to transpose into a Scheveningen or a Dragon with 6...e6 or 6...g6 respectively. Failing that, he might well consider Murey's 6...♕b6.

White should be careful to avoid playing ♗f1-g2 followed by f2-f3, as he would need to play the loosening f3-f4 in order to then rejuvenate the bishop. In order to do this he should be willing to play Pilnik's 8 ♘xc6.

CHAPTER THREE

The Scheveningen Variation

The Scheveningen formation, in which Black plays ...e7-e6 and ...d7-d6, can arise from many different move orders. Direct transpositions are possible from the Classical, Najdorf, Paulsen and Kan Variations, which makes this one of the most important chapters in the book.

Black's most common set-up involves delaying ...♘c6 as in Games 14-17. White's most direct way of meeting this is by advancing his kingside pawns with f2-f4, g2-g4 and g4-g5 etc. as in Popovic-Dizdarevic (Game 14) and Movsesian-Rublevsky (Game 15). Of these two games, Popovic's play looks more measured and effective to me.

White can also try to inhibit Black's queenside counterplay with 9 a4 before advancing on the kingside, and this is how White played it in Kagan-Csom (Game 16). Although White lost this game, it was not because of the actual opening. The idea of doubling major pieces on the h-file is in my view quite mistaken. White should advance his h-pawn up the board before deciding how to deploy his pieces.

White's most positional way of playing is seen in Peng Xiaomin-Akesson (Game 17), in which White sets about obtaining a grip on the position by playing for c2-c4 after ♘xc6 and ♘c3-a4, gaining a tempo by threatening ♘a4-b6. This does not mean that he is abandoning the plan of advancing on the kingside; it is simply delayed in favour of the short-term suppression of Black's programmed counterplay.

In Ivanov-De Firmian (Game 18) Black sidesteps White's strategy with 9...♖b8, only to be hit tactically with ♘xc6 and e4-e5 because of the rook's new position. Mokry-Marjanovic (Game 19) features a delay in Black playing ...♘g8-f6 so as to take the sting out of e4-e5. In Popovic-Short (Game 20) and Lau-Razuvaev (Game 21) Black achieves the same objective by playing an early ...♗c8-d7, though the disadvantage of this is that Black's queen's bishop is rather passively played should White go back to the plan of advancing his kingside pawns.

As the Russian saying goes, it's better

to be beautiful, healthy and rich than ugly, ill and poor. You cannot have everything.

Game 14
Popovic-Dizdarevic
Sarajevo 1982

---

1 e4 c5 2 ♘f3 d6 3 ♘c3 ♘f6 4 d4 cxd4 5 ♘xd4 e6 6 g3 a6 7 ♗g2 ♕c7

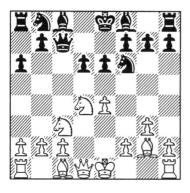

8 0-0 ♗e7 9 f4

Commencing a forthright strategy of a pawn storm on the kingside. For 9 ♗e3 see Game 17, whilst 9 a4 is featured in Game 16.

9...0-0

After an immediate 9...♘c6 White can play 10 ♘xc6 bxc6 11 e5. Tal-Darga, Hamburg 1960 continued 11...dxe5 12 fxe5 ♘d7 13 ♗f4 0-0 14 ♘e4!? ♗b7 (after 14...♘xe5 White should play 15 ♔h1, preventing Black from unpinning his knight with ...♕b6+ and leaving him in an awkward situation) 15 ♕h5 g6 16 ♕e2 c5 (16...♘xe5 17 ♔h1, intending 18 ♖ae1, again looks awkward for Black) 17 ♘f6+ ♗xf6 18 exf6 e5 19 ♗xe5 ♘xe5 20 ♗xb7 and White won a pawn.

10 g4

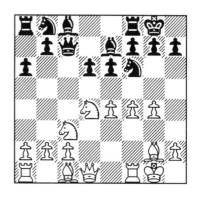

10...♘c6 11 ♘xc6 bxc6 12 g5 ♘e8

Black has also played 12...♘d7. Play continues 13 f5 ♖e8 (13...f6!? 14 g6 h6 15 ♕h5 ♘e5 16 ♗f4 ♖d8 17 ♖ae1 ♗f8 18 ♔h1 exf5 19 exf5 ♗b7 20 ♖e3 looked dangerous for Black in Mololkin-Kudrjavcev, Russia 1995) 14 f6 ♗f8 (14...gxf6 15 gxf6 ♘xf6 16 ♗g5 ♘d7 17 ♖xf7!! ♗xg5 18 ♕h5 ♘f6 19 ♕xg5+ ♔xf7 20 e5!

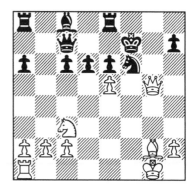

led to a brilliant win for White in Malinin-Chochlov, correspondence 1991 as 20...dxe5 is refuted by 21 ♖f1 ♕e7 22 ♘e4 etc.) 15 fxg7 ♗xg7 16 ♗f4 ♘e5 (Malinin has also analysed a couple of alternatives as being good for White: 16...♕b6+ 17 ♔h1 ♕xb2 18 ♕h5! ♖f8 19 ♗xd6 ♕xc3 20 ♗xf8 ♗xf8 21 ♕xf7+

♔h8 22 e5 ♕xe5 23 ♗xc6 ♖b8 24 ♖ad1; and 16...e5 17 ♗e3 ♘f8 18 ♘a4 ♖b8 19 c4, intending 20 c5) 17 ♗xe5 ♗xe5 18 ♕h5 ♕e7 19 ♖f3 ♕f8 20 ♖af1 ♖a7 21 ♘d1 and White was developing a very strong attack in Campora-Timman, Biel 1995.

13 ♗e3

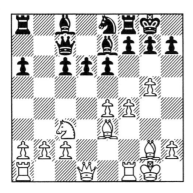

A solid developing move. For 13 ♔h1 see the next game.

13...♖b8 14 b3 d5 15 f5 ♗d6 16 fxe6 fxe6?!

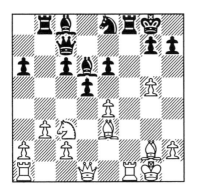

Attempting to improve on the 16...♗xh2+ of Popovic-Stoica, Tuzla 1981, which was promising for White after 17 ♔h1 ♗e5 18 exf7+ ♖xf7 19 ♕d3 ♘d6 20 ♗d4. Dizdarevic's line does in fact seem worse.

17 ♖xf8+ ♗xf8 18 ♕f3 ♘d6 19 ♖f1 ♘f7 20 ♔h1 ♗b7 21 h4 g6 22 ♗b6 ♕d7 23 ♘a4 ♗g7 24 ♘c5

With White's pieces arriving on beautiful squares, he has a clear advantage.

24...♕e7 25 ♕g3 ♖e8

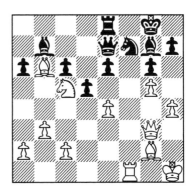

After 25...e5 one good move would be 26 ♘d3.

26 ♘xb7 ♕xb7 27 ♗c5 ♘e5 28 exd5 exd5 29 ♖e1 ♕f7 30 ♖f1 ♕b7 31 ♕f4 ♘f7 32 c4 ♕d7 33 cxd5 cxd5 34 ♕f3 ♖e4 35 ♕f2 ♖e8 36 ♗d4 ♘e5 37 ♕g3 ♘g4 38 ♗xg7 ♔xg7 39 ♗h3 ♖e4 40 ♗xg4 1-0

Black gets mated after 40 ♗xg4 ♖xg4 (or 40...♕xg4 41 ♕c7+) 41 ♕e5+ ♔g8 42 ♕b8+.

Game 15
Movsesian-Rublevsky
Polanica Zdroj 1996

1 e4 c5 2 ♘f3 e6 3 ♘c3 a6 4 d4 cxd4 5 ♘xd4 ♕c7 6 g3 ♘f6 7 ♗g2 ♗e7 8 0-0 0-0 9 f4 d6 10 g4 ♘c6 11 ♘xc6 bxc6 12 g5 ♘e8 13 ♔h1

Besides this move and 13 ♗e3 (see the previous game) White has also played the immediate 13 f5, though this allows Black to free his position with

13...exf5 14 exf5 d5 with an excellent game.

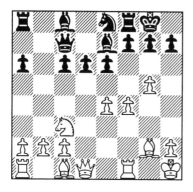

13...♖b8 14 ♘e2 f6 15 gxf6 ♘xf6 16 c4 d5 17 e5 ♘e4 18 ♘g3 ♘c5 19 b3

19 ♕c2? allows Black to seize the initiative with 19...dxc4 20 ♕xc4 a5 followed by ...♗a6.

19...dxc4 20 bxc4 ♖d8 21 ♕c2 ♗d7 22 ♗e3 ♗e8 23 ♕f2!?

After the 'natural' 23 ♘e4 Black would set up a nasty pin with 23...♗g6.

23...♘d3 24 ♕f3 ♔h8

24...♗g6? is met by 25 ♗h3!, but now Black would meet 25 ♗h3 with 25...♗d7 followed by ...c6-c5.

25 ♕g4 ♗c5 26 ♗xc5 ♘xc5 27 f5?

This looks aggressive but it leaves the

e-pawn weak. White should settle for 27 ♘e4 ♘xe4 28 ♗xe4 with approximate equality.

27...exf5 28 ♘xf5 ♗g6 29 ♘d6

29 ♘d4 is strongly met by 29...♖b2! as after 30 e6 there follows 30...♗e4! 31 e7 (31 ♗xe4? ♕xh2 mate) 31...♕xe7 32 ♗xe4 ♘xe4 33 ♘xc6 ♕d6, threatening mate on h2.

29...♘d3?

Missing White's clever reply. Black should hit the e-pawn with 29...♕e7!, and only after 30 ♕g3 play 30...♘d3!.

30 c5!

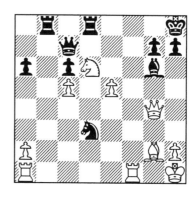

30...♘xc5

And not 30...♘xe5? 31 ♕g3 ♘d3 32 ♘f7+ winning the queen.

31 ♖ad1 ♕e7 32 ♕d4 ♘e6 33 ♕c4 c5 34 ♖f2?

Too ambitious. White should take his pawn back with 34 ♕xa6.

34...♘g5 35 ♕d5 c4?

Giving White yet another chance. Better is 35...h6, so as to meet 36 h4 with 36...♘h7.

36 ♖df1?

The final mistake, after which Black finishes the game with great precision. White should restore the material balance with 36 h4 ♘e6 37 ♕xc4 as after

37...a5 (threatening ...罩b4) he can play 38 a3.

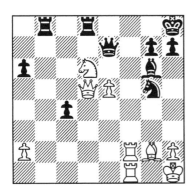

36...c3 37 豐c5 c2 38 ⊘f7+

After 38 罩xc2 ⊈xc2 39 ⊘f7+ 豐xf7 40 罩xf7 ⊘xf7 41 豐xc2 ⊘xe5 Black's two rooks would be more than a match for White's queen.

38...豐xf7 39 罩xf7 ⊘xf7 40 e6 罩bc8! 41 exf7

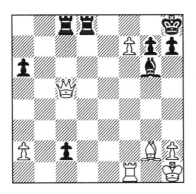

After 41 e7 Rublevsky gives 41...罩e8 42 豐a3 罩xe7? (42...罩c7 is better) as winning for Black, but this seems wrong because of 43 豐xe7 c1豐 44 罩xc1 罩xc1+ 45 ⊈f1, when 45...罩xf1+? 46 ⊈g2 actually wins for White!

41...⊈xf7 42 豐g1 ⊈h5 43 ⊈e4 ⊈e2! 44 ⊈xc2 ⊈xf1 45 ⊈b3 ⊈h3 46 豐e3 罩e8 47 豐xh3

Or 47 豐d2 罩f8 etc.

47...罩c1+ 0-1

Game 16
Kagan-Csom
Sao Paulo 1973

1 e4 c5 2 ⊘f3 d6 3 d4 cxd4 4 ⊘xd4 ⊘f6 5 ⊘c3 a6 6 g3 e6 7 ⊈g2 豐c7 8 0-0 ⊈e7 9 a4

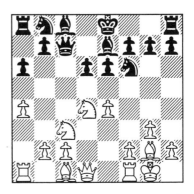

A quiet approach that aims to inhibit Black's queenside counterplay before pursuing White's own plans on the kingside.

9...⊘c6 10 ⊘b3 b6!

It is important for Black to play this now. After 10...0-0 White can play 11 a5.

11 f4

White can also start his pawn storm with 11 g4 but this probably leads to much the same kind of play. The move 11...罩b8 looks playable, while Bjerring-Eingorn, Copenhagen 1988 continued 11...⊈b7 12 g5 ⊘d7 13 f4 0-0 14 豐h5 (White may consider 14 h4!? or 14 罩f3) 14...罩fe8 15 f5 ⊘de5 with Black re-grouping nicely on the kingside.

The spectacular 11 e5 dxe5 12 ⊘b5 was tried in Barendregt-Vasiukov, Amsterdam 1969 but led to the better game for Black after 12...axb5 13 axb5 ♖xa1 14 ♗xc6+ ♗d7 15 ♗xd7+ ♘xd7 16 ♘xa1 0-0 due to Black having the more dangerous pawn majority.

11...♖b8

Aiming for ...b6-b5. Black's alternative is to regroup his pieces with 11...♗b7, when play might continue 12 ♗e3 0-0 13 ♕e2 ♖fe8 14 ♖ad1 ♖ac8 15 g4 ♘d7 16 g5 ♗f8 17 h4!? (Black can defend himself after both 17 ♖f3 ♘b4 18 ♖h3 g6 19 ♕f2 ♗g7 20 ♖d2 ♖e7 as in De Firmian-Hernandez Gilberto, Linares 1994; and 17 ♕f2 ♘b4 18 ♖d2 ♘c5 19 ♘xc5 bxc5 as in Kovalev-Jansa, Gausdal 1990) 17...♘a5! 18 ♘d4 ♘c4 19 ♗c1 e5! 20 ♘f5 exf4 21 ♖xf4 ♘ce5 22 ♔h1 ♘c5 23 ♘e3 ♘g6 24 ♖g4 ♘e6 as in Donguines-Sandler, Genting 1995. Now 25 ♖f1 is the best according to Sandler. My own preference would be for White thanks to his extra space and grip on d5, though Black's position is certainly not bad.

12 ♗e3

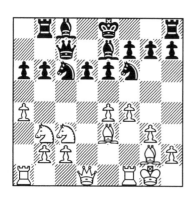

The immediate 12 g4 is certainly worth considering, having been played by Hjartarson against Gheorghiu in the 1984 Thessaloniki Olympiad. The game

concluded 12...♘d7 13 g5 g6 14 f5 ♘de5 15 fxe6 fxe6 16 ♕e2 ♘f7 17 h4 0-0 18 ♗e3 ♘fe5 19 ♘d4 ♘xd4 20 ♗xd4 ♕c4 21 ♕d2 ♕c7 22 ♕e2 ♕c4 23 ♕d2 ♕c7 ½-½.

12...0-0

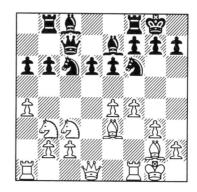

In Kobese-Lautier, Las Vegas 1999 Black played 12...♘a5 which is best met by 13 ♘d2 (in the game White played 13 e5 but after 13...♘d7 14 exd6 ♗xd6 15 ♘e4 ♘c4 his initiative fizzled out).

13 g4 ♘d7 14 g5 ♖e8 15 ♕h5?!

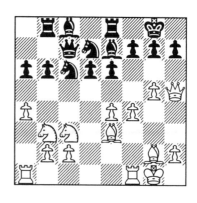

Doubling on the h-file fails to produce the desired results and in many cases leaves White's major pieces misplaced. If White really wants to operate on the h-file like this he should probably do so with 15 ♖f3.

A much better plan is to leave the kingside pawns free to advance by playing 15 h4, when 15...♗f8 16 h5 cramps Black's kingside whilst keeping White's options open with his pieces.

15...b5

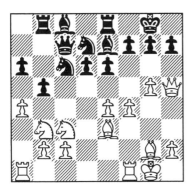

Alternatively Black can shore up his kingside with 15...g6 as in Al Modiahki-Suba, Manila Olympiad 1992, after which White impaled himself upon Black's rock-like defence with 16 ♕h4 ♗b7 17 f5 ♘de5 18 fxe6 fxe6 19 ♗h3 ♗f8 20 ♖f6 but had no compensation for the exchange following 20...♗g7 21 ♖af1 ♗xf6 22 gxf6 ♗c8 etc.

16 axb5 axb5 17 f5 g6 18 ♕h3 ♗f8 19 ♖f4 b4 20 ♖h4 h5! 21 fxg6 fxg6 22 ♘e2 e5 23 ♖xh5?!

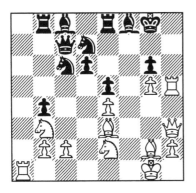

A desperate sacrifice, against which Black easily defends. But otherwise the rook is badly misplaced.

23...gxh5 24 ♕xh5 ♖e7 25 ♖f1 ♗a6 26 ♘g3

More material goes on to the bonfire, but with two rooks against a bishop Black can afford to give some back.

26...♗xf1 27 ♗xf1 ♖h7 28 ♕g4 ♘e7 29 g6 ♘xg6!

And not 29...♖g7 30 ♕e6+ ♔h8 31 ♕h3+ when White draws by repetition. The remainder of the game consists of White making one-move threats. Black, in turn, has one-move defences.

30 ♕xg6+ ♔h8 31 ♘d2 ♘b6 32 ♘f3 ♕g7 33 ♕e6 ♗e7 34 ♗xb6 ♖xb6 35 ♗c4 ♖b8 36 ♔g2 ♖f8 37 ♗d5 ♖h6 38 ♕d7 ♖hf6 39 ♘h4 ♖f2+ 40 ♔h3 ♗xh4 41 ♕xd6 ♕h7 42 ♔g4 ♖8f4+ 0-1

Game 17
Peng Xiaomin-Akesson
Yerevan Olympiad 1996

---

1 e4 c5 2 ♘f3 e6 3 d4 cxd4 4 ♘xd4 ♘f6 5 ♘c3 d6 6 g3 a6

This position can naturally arise from a Najdorf move order in which Black meets 6 g3 with 6...e6.

7 ♗g2 ♗e7 8 0-0 ♕c7 9 ♗e3

A strategic treatment that plans to control the centre before taking action on the kingside.

9...♘c6

It may be slightly more precise to play 9...0-0 as after 10 f4 ♘c6 11 ♘xc6 bxc6 12 ♘a4 White is then committed to f2-f4.

a) Kudrin-Gobet, St. Martin 1991 continued 12...♗b7 13 c4 c5 14 ♘c3 ♘d7 15 ♖c1 ♖ad8 16 g4 ♘b8 17 g5 f5 18 ♕e2 ♖de8 19 exf5 ♗xg2 20 ♕xg2 ♖xf5 21 ♖cd1 with the better game for White because of Black's hanging pawns on e6 and d6.

b) 12...♖b8 13 c4 c5 (13...d5 14 e5 ♘e4 15 ♖c1 ♕a5 16 b3 gave White an edge in Sax-Plachetka, Balatonbereny 1985) 14 g4 ♗b7 15 ♘c3 ♘d7 16 g5 f5! (after 16...♖fe8 White can start an attack with 17 ♖f3) 17 ♕c2 ♘b6 18 b3 fxe4 19 ♗xe4 ♗xe4 20 ♕xe4 ♕d7 21 ♖ad1 ♖f5! was Kaidanov-Yermolinsky, US Championship 1994.

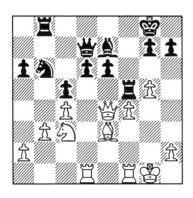

Now Kaidanov analysed 22 ♕g2 (in the game he played the dubious 22 ♘e2) 22...d5 23 ♘e4 ♖c8 24 ♘g3 ♖ff8 25 f5 exf5 26 cxd5 ♗d6 27 ♘h5! with chances

for both sides.

10 ♘xc6! bxc6 11 ♘a4 ♗b7

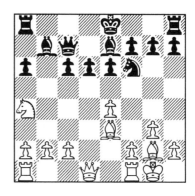

Alternatively Black can play 11...♖b8 12 c4 c5 13 b3 (the less subtle 13 f4 would transpose into the previous note) 13...0-0 14 ♘c3 ♗b7 (Black should play 14...♘d7 followed by 15...♗f6) 15 g4 ♖fe8 16 g5 ♘d7 17 f4 (played when Black is no longer geared up to answer this with ...f7-f5) 17...♗f8 18 ♕d2 ♖bd8 19 ♖ad1 ♘b8 20 ♖f3 ♘c6 21 ♖h3 g6 22 f5 and White had a powerful attack in Al.Ivanov-Fedorowicz, Chicago 1991.

12 ♗b6

This is much more incisive than 12 c4 c5 13 ♘c3 ♘d7 14 f4 ♗f6 as in Kudrin-Velikov, Belgrade 1988.

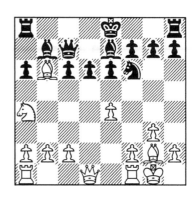

12...♕b8 13 e5 dxe5 14 ♗c5 ♕c7

15 ♖e1!

A novelty. Previously White had played 15 ♕f3.

15...♕a5

If 15...♘d7?! there follows 16 ♗xe7 ♔xe7 17 ♕g4, threatening 18 ♕b4+.

16 ♗xe7 ♔xe7 17 b3 ♖hd8

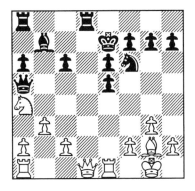

18 ♕c1!

The queen intends to re-emerge on either the a3- or the g5-square.

18...♖ab8

If 18...♘d7 there is 19 ♕a3+ ♔e8 20 ♖ed1 followed by 21 ♖d6 and 22 ♖ad1 with very strong pressure.

19 ♕g5 h6 20 ♕xe5

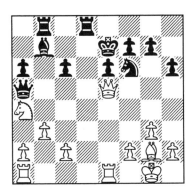

Recovering the pawn with a clear advantage in the endgame. After 20 ♕xg7? the tables would be turned with

20...♖h8 followed by 21...♖bg8.

20...♕xe5 21 ♖xe5 ♖d2 22 ♖c5 ♘d7 23 ♖c3 c5? 24 ♘xc5?

This allows Black to obtain enough counterplay to draw. The right way was 24 ♗xb7 ♖xb7 25 ♘xc5, after which 25...♖c7 26 ♖d3 ♖xd3 27 ♘xd3 ♖c2 28 ♘b4 ♖b2 29 ♘xa6 ♘e5 30 ♘b4 ♘g4 31 ♖f1 is possible because White's king is not on g2 (31...♘e3+ is not possible).

24...♖c8 25 ♖d3 ♖xd3 26 ♘xd3 ♗xg2 27 ♔xg2 ♖xc2 28 ♘b4 ♖b2 29 ♘xa6 ♘e5 30 b4

With White's king on g2 it is bad to play 30 ♘b4 because of 30...♘g4 31 ♘d3 (31 ♖f1? ♘e3+) 31...♖d2 32 h3 ♘e3+ 33 ♔f3 ♘d1 etc.

30...♘d3 31 a4

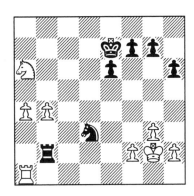

31...♖xf2+

31...♘xb4 32 ♘xb4 ♖xb4 33 a5 ♖b7 34 a6 ♖a7 35 ♔f3 ♔d6 36 ♔e4 f6! should draw.

32 ♔g1 ♖b2 33 b5 e5 34 ♘c7 e4 35 a5 ♘e5 36 ♖a3 ♖b1+ 37 ♔f2 ♖b2+ 38 ♔f1 ♘c4 39 a6 ♔d7 40 a7 ♖b1+ 41 ♔g2 ♖b2+ 42 ♔h3 ♘b6 43 ♖a6 1-0

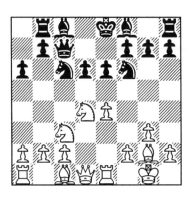

Game 18
Al.Ivanov-De Firmian
US Championship, Salt Lake City 1999

---

1 e4 c5 2 ♘f3 d6 3 d4 cxd4 4 ♘xd4 ♘f6 5 ♘c3 a6 6 g3 e6 7 ♗g2 ♕c7 8 0-0 ♘c6 9 ♖e1 ♖b8

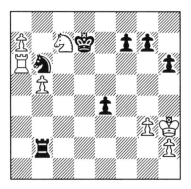

If Black wants to put his bishop on

d7 it is better that he does it without first putting his queen on c7. In this position 9...♗d7 is met by 10 ♘xc6 bxc6 (after 10...♗xc6 White plays 11 ♘d5! ♕d8 12 ♗g5 with advantage) 11 ♘a4 ♖b8 (neither does Black escape the problems associated with this kind of pawn structure after 11...♖d8 12 c4 c5 13 ♗f4 ♗e7 14 e5 dxe5 15 ♗xe5 as in J.Polgar-Milos, Sao Paulo 1996; or 11...e5 12 c4 ♗e7 13 c5 as in Tal-Najdorf, Belgrade 1970) 12 c4 c5 13 ♘c3 ♗e7 14 ♗f4 e5 (14...0-0 15 e5 ♘e8 16 ♘e4 dxe5 17 ♗xe5 ♕xe5 18 ♕xd7 was also good for White in Yakovich-Lukov, Cappelle la Grande 1996) 15 ♗c1 0-0 16 h3 ♗e6 17 b3 ♕d7 18 ♔h2 ♘e8 19 f4 f6 20 ♗e3 ♕c6 21 g4 and White was clearly better in Grünfeld-Votava, Rishon le Zion 1992.

10 ♘xc6 bxc6 11 e5! dxe5 12 ♖xe5 ♗d6

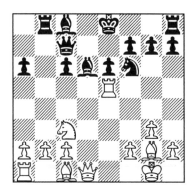

White has the same kind of edge after 12...♕xe5 13 ♗f4 ♕c5 14 ♗xb8 due, once again, to his superior pawn structure. Topalov-J.Polgar, Vienna 1996 continued 14...♗e7 15 ♗f4 0-0 16 ♘a4 ♕b5 17 b3 e5 18 c4 ♕b8 19 ♗e3 with an edge for White, though Black managed to hold a draw.

13 ♖e2

White can also play 13 ♖e1, which leaves room for the queen on e2 but loses the possibility of easily doubling rooks on the d-file. Play might continue 13...0-0 14 b3 c5 (14...♖d8 15 ♕e2 ♗b7 16 ♘a4 ♘d7 17 ♗g5 ♖e8 18 ♖ad1 was slightly better for White in Leko-Movsesian, Las Vegas 1999) 15 ♗b2 (15 ♘e4!?) 15...♖d8 16 ♕e2 ♗b7 17 ♘e4 ♘xe4 18 ♗xe4 ♗xe4 19 ♕xe4, and now 19...c4! was an equaliser in Adams-Lautier, Munich 1993.

13...0-0 14 b3 c5 15 ♗g5!?

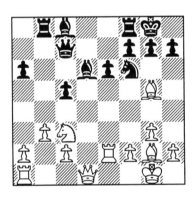

A much more aggressive post for the bishop than the obvious b2-square, though not necessarily better. A game Adams-Emms, Southend 2000 continued 15 ♗b2 ♗b7 16 ♗xb7 ♖xb7 17 ♘e4 ♘xe4 18 ♖xe4 ♖d8 19 ♕e2 with a small but clear advantage for White due to Black's weakened queenside pawns and bad bishop.

15...♗b7 16 ♗xb7 ♖xb7 17 ♕d3 ♕c6

It was worth considering 17...c4!?, sacrificing a pawn in order to break up White's pawn structure.

18 ♗xf6 gxf6 19 ♘e4 ♗e7 20 ♕c3 f5 21 ♘f6+ ♗xf6 22 ♕xf6 ♖d7 23

♖d2 ♖fd8 24 ♕xd8+ ♖xd8 25 ♖xd8+ ♔g7 26 ♖e1 h5 27 h4 f4 28 ♖d3 fxg3

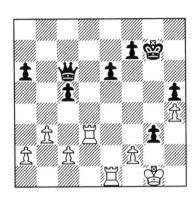

29 ♖xg3+

It White tries to keep his pawn structure intact with 29 fxg3 there follows 29...c4! 30 ♖c3 ♕d6 (threatening 31...♕d4+) 31 ♖ee3 ♕d1+ which draws by repetition.

29...♔f8 30 ♖d3 ♕c7 31 ♖e4 ♔e7 32 ♖f3 ♕d8 33 ♖d3 ♕h8 34 a4 ♕h7 35 ♖c4 ♕f5 36 ♔f1 ♕e5 37 ♖e3 ♕d5 38 ♔e2 f5 39 ♖d3 ♕e5+ 40 ♔f1 ♔f6 41 ♖e3 ♕d5

An interesting alternative is 41...♕h2, intending 42...f4, with quite dangerous counterplay.

42 ♔e2 e5?!

This kind of position is very difficult to defend for Black, and this looks like a mistake. A better try is 42...♕h1!?, after which 43 ♖xc5 f4 44 ♖ee5 ♕xh4 45 ♖xh5 ♕g4+ 46 ♔d2 ♕g2 47 ♔e2 ♕g4+ results in a draw by repetition.

43 ♖d3 ♕c6

In this position 43...♕h1 is less effective as after 44 ♖xc5 f4 Black no longer attacks a rook.

44 f3! f4 45 ♔d2 ♔f5 46 ♖e4 ♕a8 47 ♔c3 ♕g8 48 ♔b2 ♔f6?

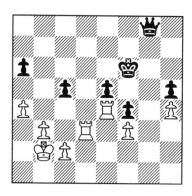

After this White slowly but surely grinds his way to victory. Black can keep some practical chances with 48...♕g3 49 ♖d5 ♕xf3 50 ♖exe5+ ♔g4 51 ♖xh5 c4, breaking up White's king position.

49 ♖d6+ ♔f5 50 ♖h6 ♕f7 51 ♖xa6 ♕e7 52 ♖c6 ♕xh4 53 ♖xc5 ♕f6 54 a5 h4 55 ♖cxe5+ ♔g6 56 a6 h3 57 a7 ♕h8 58 ♖e1 h2 59 c3 ♕a8 60 ♖5e2 ♕xa7 61 ♖xh2 ♕d7 62 ♖e4 ♔g5 63 ♖g2+ ♔f5 64 ♖d4 ♕e6 65 ♖gd2 ♕e1 66 ♖d5+ ♔f6 67 b4 ♕f1 68 ♖2d3 ♕e2+ 69 ♔b3 ♕f1 70 b5 ♔e7 71 ♔b4 ♕f2 72 c4 ♕g1 73 ♖5d4 ♕b1+ 74 ♔c5 ♕a1 75 ♖e4+ ♔f6 76 ♖xf4+ ♔e5 77 ♖e4+ ♔f5 78 ♖d5+ ♔f6 79 ♖f4+ ♔e6 80 ♖e4+

♔f6 81 ♖ed4 ♕a3+ 82 ♔b6 ♕xf3 83 c5 1-0

Game 19
Mokry-Marjanovic
Trnava 1989

1 e4 c5 2 ♘f3 e6 3 d4 cxd4 4 ♘xd4 ♘c6 5 ♘c3 ♕c7 6 g3 a6 7 ♗g2 d6 8 0-0 ♗d7

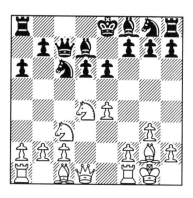

By delaying the development of his king's knight, Black hopes to take the sting out of a possible e4-e5 by White.

An alternative way of doing this, which has been championed by the Czech GM Plachetka, has been to play 8...♗e7. Then 9 ♖e1 ♖b8 10 ♘xc6 bxc6 11 e5 d5 12 ♘e2 (12 ♘a4 c5 13 c4 d4

14 b3 h5 15 h4 g6 16 ♘b2 ♘h6 was fine for Black in Popovic-Plachetka, Stara Pazova 1988) 12...c5 13 c4 d4 14 ♘f4 g6 15 ♘d3 h5 16 ♗d2 was slightly better for White in Tiviakov-Plachetka, Torcy 1991.

9 ♖e1 ♗e7 10 ♘xc6 ♗xc6

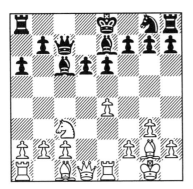

After 10...bxc6 White gained the advantage with 11 ♘a4 ♖d8 12 ♕e2 ♗c8 13 e5 d5 14 c4 in Timman-Marjanovic, Zagreb 1985 due to Black's difficulties with development and the impending pressure on the c-file.

11 ♕g4

The most dangerous move for Black, provoking a double-edged advance of his h-pawn.

The prophylactic 11 a4 is also playable but after 11...♘f6 (11...b6 is met by 12 ♕g4, which represents a slightly improved version of the game) 12 a5 0-0 13 ♗e3 ♘d7 (13...♖ac8 14 ♗b6 ♕d7 15 f4 ♗d8 16 ♗f2 b5 17 axb6 ♕b7 is also playable as in Popovic-Gufeld, Vinkovci 1982) 14 ♘a4 ♖ae8 15 ♘b6 f5 16 ♘xd7 ♕xd7 17 ♗b6 f4 Black had good counterplay in Illescas Cordoba-J.Polgar, Pamplona 1990.

11...h5

Exploiting the fact that if White cap-

tures on g7 he would lose his queen.

12 ♕e2 b5

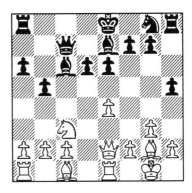

Expanding on the queenside prevents Black from becoming cramped in this sector. Alternatives include:

a) 12...♘f6 13 ♗f4 (13 a4 ♖d8 14 ♗g5 ♔f8 15 ♖ad1 ♘e8 16 ♗e3 ♘f6 17 h3 was fine for Black in Kuijf-Gheorghiu, Amsterdam 1986 as his position is rock solid) 13...h4 14 a4 ♖c8 15 a5 e5 16 ♗g5 gave White an edge in Romero-P.Cramling, Las Palmas 1991.

b) 12...h4 13 ♗d2 hxg3 14 hxg3 ♘f6 15 a4 ♖c8 16 a5 e5 17 ♖ec1 and White's position was preferable in Nunn-Van der Wiel, Rotterdam 1989.

13 ♗d2

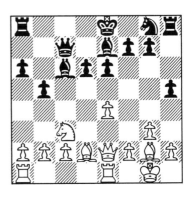

This move, intending 14 a4, is by far

the most dangerous for Black. After the quiet 13 a3 Black has a choice of good moves, my own preference being 13...♘f6.

13...h4!?

The older 13...♕b7 also seems playable, but this move's reputation took a battering in Tal-Andersson, Milan 1975: 14 a3 ♔f8?! (14...♘f6 is better) 15 ♘a2! a5 16 b4! d5 (16...a4 17 c4 bxc4 18 ♕xc4) 17 exd5 ♗xd5 18 ♗xd5 ♕xd5 19 bxa5 and Black was in serious trouble.

In his notes Tal suggested an interesting pawn sacrifice with 13...♘f6 14 ♗g5 0-0!?, though the onus is on Black to demonstrate adequate compensation after 15 ♗xf6 ♗xf6 16 ♕xh5 b4 17 ♘d1 etc.

14 a4 bxa4 15 ♘xa4 hxg3 16 hxg3 ♘f6 17 c4 ♖b8 18 b4

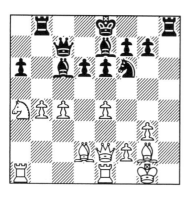

White prepares to retreat his knight to c3, but maybe this wasn't necessary. As Mokry thought that Black's 13th move was a novelty, perhaps he was unaware of a game Sax-Marjanovic, Subotica 1987, in which White played an immediate 18 ♘c3!?. After 18...♖xb2 19 ♖xa6 he had dangerous threats, the game continuing 19...♘d7 (not 19...0-0? because of 20 ♖xc6 ♕xc6 21 e5; and

19...♖b6 is well met by 20 ♘b5) 20 ♘d5! ♕b7 21 ♖aa1 ♗g5 22 ♖ed1 ♔f8? (Black might have been afraid of 22...0-0 23 ♕h5 but he can answer this with just 23...♗f6) 23 ♕e1 ♗xd2 24 ♖xd2 ♘c5 25 ♘c3 and Black's d6-pawn was weak.

18...♘d7 19 ♘c3 ♗b7 20 c5 dxc5 21 ♘d5 ♕d8 22 ♘xe7 ♕xe7 23 bxc5 ♕xc5 24 ♗f4 e5 25 ♗e3 ♕e7 26 ♖ab1 ½-½

The draw looks somewhat premature, but Mokry pointed out that a repetition was possible after 26...♗c8 (and not 26...0-0? 27 ♗a7) 27 ♕c2 (27 ♖xb8 ♘xb8 28 ♖c1 ♕b7) 27...0-0 28 ♗c5 ♖xb1 29 ♗xe7 ♖xe1+ 30 ♔h2 ♖e8 31 ♗b4 ♖a1 32 ♗c3 ♖a3 33 ♗b4 ♖a1 etc.

Game 20
Popovic-Short
Belgrade 1989

---

1 e4 c5 2 ♘f3 e6 3 d4 cxd4 4 ♘xd4 ♘c6 5 ♘c3 a6 6 g3 d6 7 ♗g2 ♗d7 8 0-0 ♘f6 9 a4 ♗e7 10 ♘b3

Preventing Black from simplifying the position with ...♘xd4 followed by ...♗c6. The bishop on d7 is now somewhat passively placed and Black must act quickly if he is not to fall victim to the coming kingside pawn storm.

10...0-0

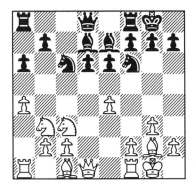

11 f4

This gives Black the possibility of a check on b6, thus making the immediate ...b7-b5 possible. In order to rule this out White can also consider 11 g4!?, when Black's main try to disturb White's plans is 11...d5. Rublevsky-Skudnov, Podolsk 1992 continued 12 exd5 ♘xd5 13 ♘xd5 exd5 14 ♗e3 ♘e5 15 h3 ♗c6 and now 16 ♘d4 seems like the most logical move

11...b5!?

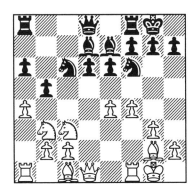

Energetic and logical, though the game continuation looks rather hairy.

Black can also proceed along more solid lines, for example 11...♖b8 12 ♕e2 (12 g4!?) 12...♘a5 13 ♘xa5 ♕xa5 14 ♗d2 ♕c7 15 ♗e3 ♗c6 16 a5 ♘d7 17 ♖fd1 ♖bc8 18 ♕d2 ♖fe8 was okay for Black in Hellers-Polugaevsky, Biel 1989. Also possible is 11...♖c8 12 ♗e3 (12 a5!? is worth considering so as to inhibit Black's queenside play) 12...b6 13 g4 ♗e8 14 ♕e2 ♘b4 15 ♖ad1 ♘d7 as in Tomescu-Loginov, Saint Vincent 1999.

12 axb5 ♕b6+ 13 ♔h1 axb5 14 ♖xa8 ♖xa8 15 e5 ♘e8 16 f5! ♖d8!

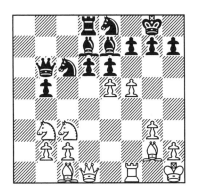

Black gets out of the long diagonal pin as soon as he can. White can answer 16...exf5 with the powerful 17 ♗f4.

17 exd6

There was another interesting and dangerous possibility in 17 f6!? gxf6 18 exf6 ♗xf6 19 ♘e4 with attacking chances for the sacrificed pawn. Popovic tries to keep it clear and simple.

17...♘xd6 18 fxe6 fxe6

18...♗xe6 allows the strong 19 ♘d5.

19 ♕e2 ♘c4 20 ♖d1?!

A rather pedestrian move which fails to meet the demands of the position. White should centralise his knights with 20 ♘e4! ♘6e5 21 c3! b4 22 ♘d4 bxc3 23 bxc3, when his nicely placed pieces give him the better game.

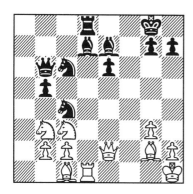

20...🨾6e5 21 🨾d4

White was possibly under the impression that Black's next move was impossible. 21 🨾e4 is better, but less effective than on the previous move.

21...🨾e8! 22 🨾f3

Originally White may have intended 22 🨾xe6? ♛xe6 23 ♜xd8 ♝xd8 24 ♝d5 but only now realised that 24...♝c6 would be a good reply.

22...♝h5 23 b3 ♝xf3 24 ♝xf3 🨾xf3 25 ♜xd8+ ♝xd8 26 ♛xf3 🨾e5 27 ♛e4 ♝f6

With time-trouble looming Black misses 27...♛f2!, after which 28 ♛e2 would be about equal.

28 ♝e3 ♛a6 29 ♝g1 🨾f7 30 🨾e2 g6 31 🨾f4 ♝e5 32 🨾d3 🨾g5 33 ♛g2 ♝d6 34 h4 🨾f7 35 ♝d4

White in turn misses the best way. 35 ♝c5 would keep the pressure up.

35...♛c8 36 ♚h2 e5 37 ♝g1?!

And here he should play 37 ♝e3 so that after 37...♛f5 38 ♛c6 e4 White can answer with 39 🨾f4.

37...♛f5 38 🨾c5 ♝xc5 39 ♝xc5 e4 40 ♝e3 🨾e5 41 ♝f4??

A blunder. With queen and knight operating on the light squares around his kingside, the position is certainly

dangerous for White. But he can hold the position comfortably enough with 41 ♛e2 followed by 42 ♚g2.

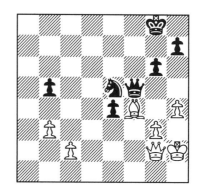

41...🨾f3+ 42 ♚h1 🨾xh4!

Winning a pawn. And once in the driver's seat, Short makes no mistake.

43 ♛e2 g5! 44 ♝b8 🨾f3 45 ♚g2 h5! 46 ♛d1 h4 47 gxh4 gxh4 48 c4 h3+ 49 ♚h1 bxc4 50 ♛d8+ ♚f7 51 bxc4 e3 52 ♛c7+ ♚g6 53 ♛b6+ ♚h5 54 ♛b5 ♚g4 55 ♛xf5+ ♚xf5 56 ♝a7 e2 57 ♝f2 ♚e4 0-1

Game 21
Lau-Razuvaev
Dortmund 1985

1 e4 c5 2 🨾f3 e6 3 d4 cxd4 4 🨾xd4

♘f6 5 ♘c3 d6 6 g3 ♘c6 7 ♗g2 ♗d7
8 0-0 ♗e7 9 ♘b3 0-0 10 g4!

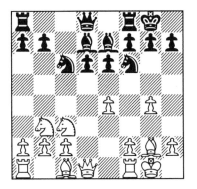

The omission of the moves ...a7-a6 and a2-a4 has a number of effects. One of them is that Black need not worry about White targeting the b6-square with a4-a5 and ♗c1-e3. Another is that 10 f4?! can be met by 10...b5! as 11 ♘xb5? ♕b6+ 12 ♘5d4 e5 wins a knight.

10...♖c8

Though it has been played by Ulf Andersson, attempting to inhibit White's kingside pawn storm with 10...h6 looks dubious to me, and some of the existing analysis also looks very suspicious. 11 ♔h1 looks like an interesting alternative as the king is often well placed on this square. However, the main line runs 11 f4 b5 12 e5 dxe5 13 g5 hxg5 14 fxg5 ♘h7 (Lautier-Andersson, Monaco {rapid} 1997 varied with 14...♘d5 but after 15 ♘xd5 exd5 16 ♕xd5 ♖c8 17 c3 White's active pieces gave him some pressure) 15 ♘e4 ♘d4 16 ♘xd4 exd4 17 ♕h5 (it might well be that the simple 17 ♕xd4 is White's best, with chances of an edge because of Black's misplaced knight on h7) 17...g6 18 ♕h4 ♖c8 (and not 18...♗c6? 19 ♖f3 when White had a

winning attack, Kindermann-Lau, Budapest 1985) 19 ♖f3 (Milos mentions 19 ♘f6+ ♗xf6 20 gxf6 ♖xc2! 21 ♗g5 but this appears to be dubious because of 21...♘xg5! 22 ♕h6 ♖xg2+ 23 ♔xg2 ♗c6+ 24 ♔g1 ♘h3+ 25 ♕xh3 ♕d5, which avoids mate and leaves Black in control) 19...e5 20 ♗h3 f5 (according to Milos the only move, but the computer engine *Crafty* says that 20...♖xc2 21 ♗xd7 ♖xc1+ 22 ♖xc1 ♘xg5! is good, and I have to say that I agree!) 21 gxf6 ♗xf6 22 ♕g3 ♗g7 23 ♖xf8+ ♘xf8 24 ♕b3+ and in this complex position the players agreed to a draw in Salazar-Milos, Asuncion 1988.

Black has tried to show that White's last move was weakening by playing 10...d5?! but this leaves White with the better game after 11 exd5 ♘xd5 12 ♘xd5 exd5 13 h3 ♗e6 14 c3 ♕d7 (14...♗d6 15 f4 ♕b6+ 16 ♔h1 d4 17 ♘xd4 ♘xd4 18 ♗e3 was no better in Wedberg-Santa Torres, New York 1988) 15 f4 g6 16 ♗e3 h5 17 f5 gxf5 18 gxf5 ♗xf5 19 ♕xh5 ♗g6 20 ♕xd5 and White was a pawn up for nothing in Popovic-Ksieski, Naleczov 1984.

11 g5 ♘e8 12 f4 b5 13 a3

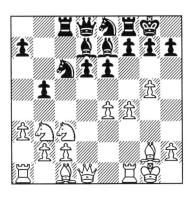

Not necessarily the best. In an earlier

game, Popovic-Stempin, Polanica Zdroj 1982, White played 13 &e3 and after 13...b4 14 ②e2 f6 15 gxf6 &xf6 16 c3 a5 17 ②bd4 bxc3 18 bxc3 White had regrouped his pieces in the centre quite nicely.

13...g6 14 &e3

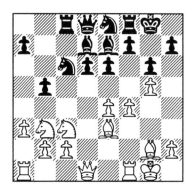

14...a6

Cautiously protecting the b5-pawn. Hübner later suggested an interesting pawn offer with 14...a5!?, after which 15 ②xb5 a4 16 ②3d4 ☐b8 gives Black compensation because of the awkward positioning of White's knights. It may be better to decline with 15 a4 bxa4 16 ②xa4.

15 ♕d2 f6 16 h4 ②g7 17 ☐ad1 &e8! 18 ②e2?!

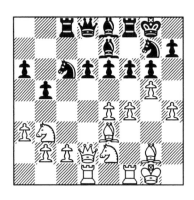

Underestimating the strength of Black's 19th move. 18 &h3!?, hitting and pinning the e-pawn, is better.

18...fxg5 19 hxg5 e5!

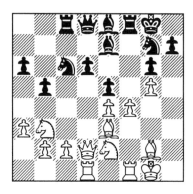

With White's knights out of touch with the d5-square, this becomes quite strong. The advance of White's kingside pawns has left his own king a bit vulnerable.

20 ②c3 exf4 21 &xf4 ②e6 22 &xd6 ☐xf1+ 23 &xf1 &xg5 24 ♕f2 &f7

And not 24...&h4? 25 &g3 &xg3 26 ☐xd8 etc.

25 ②d5 ②cd4 26 ②xd4 ♕xd6

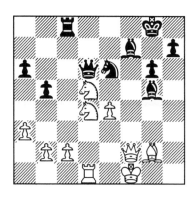

27 &h3?!

Earlier on this would have been quite correct. In this particular position, however, it is quite ineffective. 27 ②f5 would be well met by 27...♕c5, so White should have preferred 27 ♘f3!?.

27...♖f8 28 ♘f3

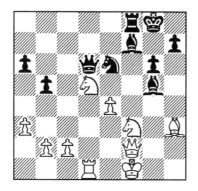

28 ♘xe6 ♗xe6 29 ♘f6+ fails because of 29...♖xf6 30 ♖xd6 ♗xh3+.

28...♘f4 29 e5

Or 29 ♘xg5 ♗xd5 30 exd5 ♘xh3 etc.

29...♕c6 30 ♗d7? ♕c4+ 31 ♔g1 ♗xd5 0-1

Summary

Black can reach the Scheveningen set-up from many different move orders and it represents a large body of chess theory. The main plan for g3 exponents is a kingside pawn storm; the bishop on g2 lends White's king protection and helps batten down the hatches in the centre lest Black tries to gain counter-play with a breakout there. But White should also be aware of Black's efforts to sidestep this plan and be ready to react accordingly. Once again we see that the idea of making the anti-positional capture on c6, which in many Sicilian lines is rather taboo, is often the best way for White to proceed. A later ♘c3-a4 and c2-c4 can establish a bind somewhat in the spirit of the English Opening.

CHAPTER FOUR

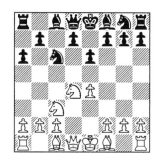

The Paulsen and Taimanov Variations

Invented by Louis and Wilfred Paulsen in the 19th century, the Paulsen Variation (1 e4 c5 2 ♘f3 e6 3 ♘c3 ♘c6 4 d4 cxd4 5 ♘xd4 a6 (or 5...♕c7 followed by 6...a6) is distinguished by its great flexibility. Black adopts a restrained position in the centre but keeps his options open as to where to put his pieces. He can expand on the queenside at some stage with ...b7-b5, switch to a Scheveningen with a later ...d7-d6 and develop his king's bishop on e7, d6, c5, b4 or even g7. The greatest exponent of the Paulsen is Mark Taimanov, who has enriched the theory in every variation.

The standard position in the 6 g3 line arises after 1 e4 c5 2 ♘f3 e6 3 ♘c3 ♘c6 4 d4 cxd4 5 ♘xd4 a6 6 g3 ♕c7 7 ♗g2 ♘f6 8 0-0, when Black must decide where to post his pieces. Black defers this decision in Nunn-Tal (Game 22) by playing 8...h6, but this may be taking flexibility a bit too far and weakens the kingside. Nunn's plan of 9 ♘b3 followed by a kingside pawn push looks quite strong. Adams-Anand (Game 23) is a highly theoretical encounter in the

8...♘xd4 and 9...♗c5 line, which represents Black's most incisive and clear-cut method of play. In this game Anand manages to draw, but only by holding an endgame in which he was a bishop for two pawns down. This is not everyone's cup of tea.

The simple 8...♗e7 looks very sensible so it is surprising how much trouble Black can get into after 9 ♖e1 ♘xd4 10 e5 as in De la Riva Aguado-Plaskett (Game 24). If Black knows of the dangers lurking here will probably play 9...0-0 (Game 25), but here too he is worse after 10 ♘xc6 dxc6 11 e5.

Another option for Black is 8...♗c5 (Game 26), which hopes for 9 ♘b3 ♗e7 followed by ...d7-d6, ...b7-b5 and ...♗b7. White's ♘d4-b3 is usually only a good plan when Black has already committed it his queen's bishop to d7.

The line which is most directly associated with Taimanov is the one in which Black plays 6...♘ge7, which has the initial aim of capturing on d4 and then bringing the e7-knight to c6. When White circumvents this plan with 7 ♘b3

(Game 27) Black will not find it easy to gain counterplay.

Game 22
Nunn-Tal
Wijk aan Zee 1982

---

1 e4 c5 2 ♘f3 e6 3 d4 cxd4 4 ♘xd4 ♘c6 5 ♘c3 a6 6 g3 ♕c7 7 ♗g2 ♘f6 8 0-0 h6

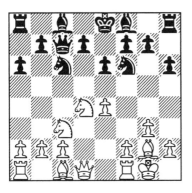

A waiting move that prevents White from posting his bishop on g5 whilst maintaining the option of capturing on d4. The drawback is that it weakens Black's kingside, a factor which can become particularly significant should he later castle short.

9 ♘b3

Ruling out the exchange on d4 and preparing to advance his kingside pawns. White can also consider 9 ♖e1 ♘xd4 10 e5!? (in the position that arises after 10 ♕xd4 ♗c5 11 ♗f4 d6 12 ♕d2 e5 Black's ...h7-h6 is more useful than White's ♖e1) but after 10...♘b5! he has to play 11 ♘xb5 (by comparison with the Game 24, Black's bishop is usefully placed on f8 in the line 11 exf6 ♘xc3 12 fxg7 ♗xg7 so White has to exchange knights) 11...axb5 12 exf6 gxf6, when

Black has quite a solid position.

9...♗e7

A natural developing move, but possibly not the best. In order to fianchetto his queen's bishop Black should probably play 9...d6 10 a4 b6 as in Pavlovic-Cabrilo, Yugoslavia 1994. That game continued 11 ♗e3 ♖b8 12 ♕e2 ♗e7 13 f4 ♘a5, after which 14 ♘d2, intending g3-g4, was probably best (in the game White played 14 ♘d4, which gave Black counterplay based on the occupation of c4).

Expanding on the queenside with 9...b5? is distinctly premature, White having a powerful answer in 10 a4 b4 11 ♘d5! exd5 12 exd5 ♘a7 13 d6! ♕b8 14 ♖e1+ ♔d8 15 ♗e3 (threatening 16 ♗xa8 ♕xa8 17 ♗b6+) 15...♘c6 16 a5 ♗b7 (and not 16...♗xd6 17 ♗b6+ ♗c7 18 ♗xc6 etc.) 17 ♗b6+ ♔c8 18 ♗c7 ♕a7, and now 19 ♕e2 ♘d8 20 ♕c4 ♘c6 21 ♘d4 is just one way to win.

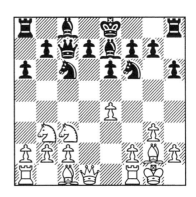

10 a4 d6 11 f4

This is one way to stop 11...b6 because of 12 e5. White can also play 11 a5, after which 11...0-0 (and not 11...b6 because of 12 axb6 ♕xb6 13 ♗e3 ♕c7 14 ♘b5 ♕b8 15 e5!) 12 ♗e3 ♘e5 13 ♗b6 ♕b8 14 ♕e2 ♘fd7 15 ♘a4 gave

White a bind in Popovic-Rajkovic, Kladovo 1980.

11...0-0

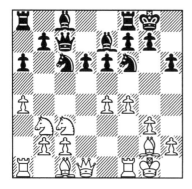

Black's king is not altogether comfortable on the kingside because of the weakness created with 8...h6. On the other hand it is difficult to see a superior alternative. In the game Popovic-Romanishin, Novi Sad 1982 Black delayed castling with 11...♗d7 but after 12 a5 b5 13 axb6 ♕xb6+ 14 ♔h1 ♖c8 15 ♕e2 ♘b4 16 ♗e3 ♕c7 17 ♘d4 found himself with the inferior game because of his weak a-pawn. Meanwhile 11...b6 is very risky because of 12 e5.

12 g4

Certainly the most direct move but not the only one. White can also prepare this advance with 12 ♗e3, for example 12...b6 13 ♕e2 ♖b8 (13...♗b7 14 g4 ♘d7 is also possible) 14 g4 ♘a5 (14...♘h7!? 15 ♖ad1 ♖e8 16 ♘d2 ♘b4 17 ♘f3 e5 18 f5 ♗b7 was also interesting in Van der Wiel-Lobron, Wijk aan Zee 1985) 15 g5 hxg5 16 fxg5 ♘h7 17 h4 ♘c4 18 ♗d4 ♗d7 19 ♖f2 b5 20 axb5 axb5 21 e5 d5 22 ♖af1 g6 23 ♘d1 b4 produced a double-edged game in Benjamin-Djuric, Hastings 1984/85

12...♗d7?

A serious mistake, after which White's kingside pawns roll on unimpeded. Black had to try 12...♘d7!, after which 13 ♗e3 b6 14 ♕e2 ♗b7 produces a tough middlegame in which both sides have chances.

13 h4!

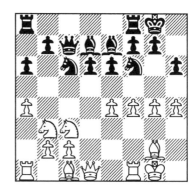

After the immediate 13 g5? hxg5 14 fxg5 ♘h7 Black would occupy the weakened e5-square. By preparing this with 13 h4, White gets ready to recapture on g5 with the h-pawn and storm down the h-file with his major pieces.

13...b5 14 g5 ♘h7

And not 14...hxg5 15 hxg5 ♘h7 because of 16 ♕h5 intending ♖f1-f3-h3.

15 ♗e3 b4 16 ♘e2

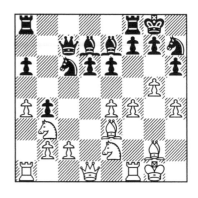

16...d5!?

With White threatening ♘g3 followed by ♕g4, Black decides to break out at any cost. The pawn sacrifice might have been more effective had Black's knight on h7 not been so badly placed. An alternative method of trying to do this was with 16...e5 but then 17 gxh6 ♗xh4 (17...gxh6 18 fxe5) 18 hxg7 ♔xg7 19 ♕d2! leaves Black's king in a perilous state.

17 exd5 exd5 18 ♕xd5 ♖ac8 19 a5!

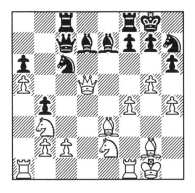

Introducing the possibility of ♗b6, which stops Black from putting a rook on d8.

19...♘b8 20 ♘ed4 ♗g4 21 ♖ae1 ♖fd8 22 ♕e4 ♖e8 23 ♗f2

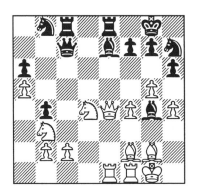

Pinning the bishop on e7 and threatening to embarrass Black's other bishop

with 24 f5.

23...♗d7 24 ♕d5 ♕d6

White was threatening 25 g6. The text move gives back the pawn, but White's mighty bishops pair soon decide matters.

25 ♘f5! ♕xd5 26 ♘xe7+ ♖xe7 27 ♗xd5 ♖xe1 28 ♖xe1 ♖xc2 29 ♖e7

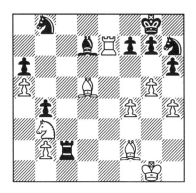

Threatening 30 g6, 30 ♗a7 and 30 ♖xf7.

29...♗c6 30 ♗xf7+ ♔f8 31 ♖c7 hxg5 32 ♗c5+ 1-0

32 ♗c5+ ♖xc5 33 ♘xc5 not only wins the exchange but threatens 34 ♘e6 mate.

Game 23
Adams-Anand
Wijk aan Zee 2001

---

1 e4 c5 2 ♘f3 e6 3 d4 cxd4 4 ♘xd4 ♘c6 5 ♘c3 ♕c7 6 g3 a6 7 ♗g2 ♘f6 8 0-0 ♘xd4

This immediate capture on d4 has been Black's most popular approach. Black gains some time for development by hitting White's centralised queen.

9 ♕xd4 ♗c5 10 ♗f4

This in turn is White's most incisive response. White makes room for his queen to drop back to d2 without blocking in his bishop.

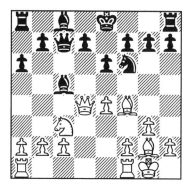

10...d6

After 10...♗xd4 11 ♗xc7 Black is very cramped in the endgame. Honfi-Kozma, Wijk aan Zee 1969 continued 11...d5 12 exd5 ♗xc3 13 bxc3 ♘xd5 14 ♗e5 f6 15 c4 ♘b4 16 ♗c3 ♘c6 17 ♖ab1 with a strong initiative thanks to the bishop pair and b-file pressure.

11 ♕d2 h6 12 ♖ad1 e5 13 ♗e3

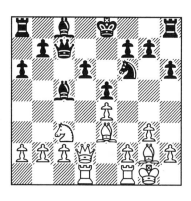

13...♗e6

At the time of writing this looks like Black's best, though there are two major alternatives:

a) 13...♗g4 14 ♗xc5 dxc5 15 f3 (after 15 ♕d6 Black holds the position with 15...♖c8) 15...♗e6 16 ♘d5 (16 f4 trans-poses into the note to White's 15th move, both sides having lost a tempo) 16...♗xd5 17 exd5 ♕d6 18 f4 trans-poses to the main game

b) 13...♗e7 is well met by 14 ♗xc5 (14 f4 is also promising, for example 14...♗g4? 15 fxe5 dxe5 16 ♖xf6 ♖ad8 17 ♖xf7+ ♔xf7 18 ♕f2+ ♔g6 19 ♗xc5 ♖xd1+ 20 ♘xd1 as in Tiviakov-Drei, Forli 1992, when Black loses material because 20...♗xd1 21 ♕f5 is mate) 14...♕xc5 15 ♘a4 ♕c6 16 f4! a5 (16...♘d7? 17 ♘c3 ♘b6 18 ♘d5+ ♘xd5 19 exd5 would give White a winning attack according to Morgado and Needleman) 17 ♕d3! b5 18 ♘c3 ♗e6 19 ♕xb5 ♕xb5 20 ♘xb5 ♗c4 21 ♘xd6 ♗xf1 22 ♘f5+ ♔f8 23 ♖xf1, leaving White with a clear advantage in Kotronias-Damljanovic, Belgrade 1993.

14 ♗xc5 dxc5 15 ♘d5

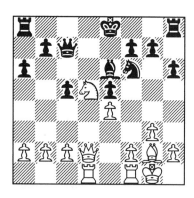

White has also tried 15 f4 0-0 and af-ter 16 ♕d6 Black has a nice resource in 16...♕a5!? which gives good play, for example:

a) 17 fxe5 ♘g4 is not to be recom-mended.

b) Adams-J.Polgar, Wijk aan Zee 2000 continued 17 ♕d2 ♖ad8 18 ♘d5 ♕xd2 19 ♖xd2 ♗xd5 20 exd5 exf4 21

♖xf4 ♘e8 and with the knight coming to d6 Black has nothing to fear.

c) 17 f5 ♗c4 18 ♖fe1 ♖fe8 19 ♕d2 ♖ad8 20 ♕e3 ♖d4 gave Black excellent counterplay in Tiviakov-Van der Sterren, Rotterdam 2000.

d) An interesting way to play the position is 17 ♕xe5 ♘g4 18 ♕h5 ♘e3 19 f5 ♗c4 20 f6 ♗xf1 21 fxg7 ♔xg7 22 ♖d6 ♖h8 23 ♗xf1 ♖h7 24 ♗d3 ♖d8 25 b4 ♕c7 26 ♕e5+ ♔g8 ½-½ as in Korneev-Fominyh, Minsk 1995.

A further possibility is 15 ♕d6 but then Black holds the balance with 15...♖c8.

15...♗xd5 16 exd5 ♕d6 17 f4 0-0 18 fxe5 ♕xe5 19 d6

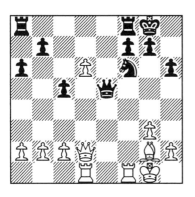

Passed pawns should be pushed, in this case before Black manages to bring his knight to d6. 19 c4 ♕d6 20 ♕f4 ♖ad8 21 ♖fe1 ♕xf4 22 gxf4 ♘e8 23 b4 b6 24 bxc5 bxc5 25 ♖e7 ♘d6 was fine for Black in Guseinov-Mehyo, Dubai 2002.

19...♕xb2 20 c4

20 ♖b1 ♕xa2 21 ♖xb7 ♖ad8 22 ♖d1 ♖fe8 23 ♕f2 ♖e5 left White's compensation looking somewhat nebulous in T.Horvath -Fominyh, Budapest 1996.

20...♕xd2 21 ♖xd2 ♖ab8 22 a4

♖fd8

The immediate 22...♘d7 also seem reasonable, Bakre-Fominyh, Cairo 2001 continuing 23 ♖b2 ♖fd8 24 ♖xb7 ♖xb7 25 ♗xb7 ♘b6 26 ♗xa6 ♘xa4 with a draw in prospect.

23 ♖b1

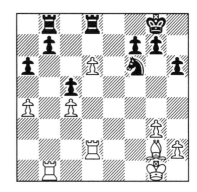

23...♘d7!

Better than 23...b6, after which Zatonskih-Alexandrova, Kramatorsk 2001 continued 24 ♖e1 ♔f8 25 ♗c6 ♖bc8 26 ♗b7 ♖b8 27 ♗xa6, recovering the single pawn deficit and maintaining the mighty passed pawn on d6.

24 ♖xb7

24 ♖e1 can be met by 24...♘b6.

24...♖xb7 25 ♗xb7 ♘e5 26 ♖d5 ♘xc4 27 ♗xa6 ♘xd6 28 a5

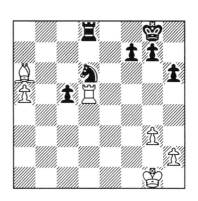

Pushing the passed pawn. Although Black is a pawn up he is fighting for a draw.

28...♔f8 29 ♗f1 ♘b7 30 ♖xd8+ ♘xd8 31 ♗g2 ♘e6 32 a6 ♘c7 33 a7 ♔e7 34 ♔f2 ♔d6 35 ♔e3 c4 36 a8♕

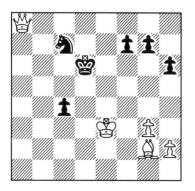

Despite the win of Black's knight it is not quite enough to take home the full point. White should be careful to avoid 36 ♔d4? ♘b5+.

36...♘xa8 37 ♗xa8 ♔e5 38 ♗f3 f5 39 ♗e2 g5 40 ♗xc4 f4+ 41 ♔f2 fxg3+ 42 hxg3 g4 43 ♗f7 ♔f6 44 ♗e8 ♔g5 45 ♔e3

45...h5 46 ♗xh5 ♔xh5 47 ♔f4 ♔h6 48 ♔xg4 ♔g6 ½-½

Keeping the 'opposition' and thus holding the draw.

Game 24
De la Riva Aguado-Plaskett
Mondariz 2000

1 e4 c5 2 ♘f3 e6 3 d4 cxd4 4 ♘xd4 ♘c6 5 ♘c3 ♕c7 6 g3 a6

6...♘f6?! 7 ♘db5 ♕b8 8 ♗f4 is known to be difficult for Black.

7 ♗g2 ♘f6 8 0-0 ♗e7 9 ♖e1 ♘xd4

In view of White's surprising reply this looks rather dubious. Black should play 9...0-0 as in Tiviakov-Adams (see the next game).

10 e5!

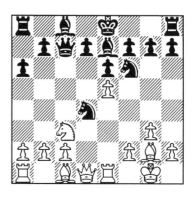

10...♘b5

Black has also tried 10...♘c6 but then 11 exf6 gxf6 (11...♗xf6 12 ♘d5 ♕d8 13 ♗e3! threatens the devastating ♗b6) 12 ♕g4 gives White more than enough for the pawn. Boudy-Lebredo, Camaguey 1985 continued 12...♘e5 13 ♕g7 ♘g6 14 ♗f4 (14 ♗e4!? is also interesting, when Renet-Marin, Bucharest 1984 led to a clear advantage for White after 14...f5 15 ♘d5 ♕a5 16 ♗f4 fxe4 17 ♘c7+ ♔d8 18 ♘xa8 etc.) 14...d6 15 ♖ad1 e5 16 ♘d5 ♕d8 17 ♗e3 ♗g4 18 ♗b6 and White went on to win.

Giving back the piece with 10...♘xc2

11 ♕xc2 ♘d5 leaves Black with a poor game after 12 ♗xd5! exd5 13 ♕d1 0-0 14 ♘xd5 ♕d8 15 ♗e3!, once again threatening ♗b6.

11 exf6!

Kindermann has pointed out that 11 ♘xb5 axb5 12 exf6 ♗xf6! is slightly better for Black.

11...gxf6

With White's knight still on the board, 11...♗xf6 can be answered by 12 ♘d5 ♕d8 13 ♗e3!, threatening 14 ♗b6. After the initial 11...♘xc3 there is 12 fxg7.

12 ♘d5!

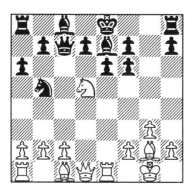

A powerful sacrifice which seems to put this line out of commission. White is also better after 12 ♘xb5 axb5 13 ♕g4 ♗f8 14 c3 as in Kindermann-Janssen, Baden-Baden 1985. But this is by no means as convincing.

12...exd5 13 ♗xd5

Threatening both 14 ♕h5 and 14 ♗xf7+ ♔xf7 15 ♕h5+.

13...h5 14 a4 ♘a7

Keeping the knight in the centre with 14...♘d6 can be strongly met by 15 ♗f4, intending ♕d4 or ♖a3-e3.

15 ♕d4 d6

After 15...♔f8 White wins with 16

♗h6+ (16 ♖xe7 ♔xe7 17 ♗g5 is also good) 16...♖xh6 17 ♕e3 etc.

16 ♕xf6 ♖f8 17 ♗g5 ♗e6 18 ♕g7!!

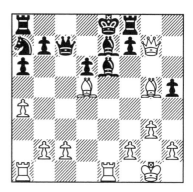

Quiet but deadly. White simply threatens to capture on e6 and power down the e-file with his rooks.

18...♗xg5

Or if 18...♗xd5 there follows 19 ♖xe7+ ♕xe7 20 ♗xe7 ♔xe7 21 ♕g5+, picking up the bishop as well.

19 ♖xe6+ ♗e7

After 19...♔d7 there follows 20 ♕xg5 fxe6 21 ♕g7+ etc.

20 ♖e4 0-0-0

20...♖d8 21 ♖ae1 ♘c8 is more tenacious, but White would still have lots of potent options such as 22 ♖f4.

21 ♖ae1 ♖de8

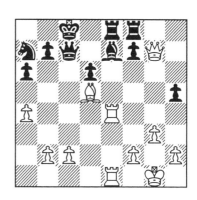

Losing on the spot, but Black's position is hopeless in any case.

22 ♖xe7! 1-0

Game 25
Tiviakov-Adams
Groningen 1993

---

1 e4 c5 2 ♘f3 e6 3 d4 cxd4 4 ♘xd4 ♘c6 5 ♘c3 ♕c7 6 g3 a6 7 ♗g2 ♘f6 8 0-0 ♗e7 9 ♖e1 0-0 10 ♘xc6 dxc6

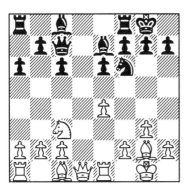

Capturing towards the centre with 10...bxc6 is also good for White after 11 e5 ♘d5 (11...♘e8 12 ♗f4 ♖b8 13 b3 left Black under serious pressure in Tringov-Doda, Leningrad 1967) 12 ♘a4 ♖b8 13 c4 ♘b6 14 ♘xb6 ♖xb6 15 ♕c2 according to Taimanov.

11 e5 ♖d8 12 ♕f3

White's best try, getting ready to recapture on c3 with the queen after Black plays ...♘d5 and ...♘xc3. This has the benefit of keeping his dark-squared bishop on the c1-h6 diagonal, from where it can help to probe Black's kingside. In an earlier encounter (Tiviakov-Rublevsky, Moscow 1991), Tiviakov played 12 ♗d2, but then 12...♘d5 13 ♕g4 ♘xc3 14 ♗xc3 b5 left White without the kingside pressure he obtains in the game.

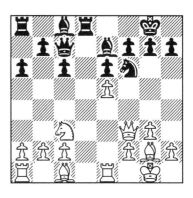

12...♘d5 13 h4

White has tried to sacrifice a pawn with 13 ♘e4 ♕xe5 14 c4 but after 14...♘f6 15 ♗g5 ♕f5 16 ♘xf6+ ♗xf6 17 ♕xf5 exf5 18 ♗xf6 gxf6 19 ♖e7 ♖b8 his initiative had fizzled out in Perenyi-Kaposztas, Salgo 1976.

13...b5

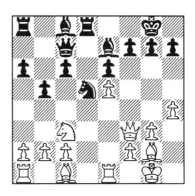

Opting to try and play actively. Simplifying the position with 13...♘xc3 14 ♕xc3 leaves White with whatever chances are going. For example, 14...♗d7 15 ♗g5 ♗e8 16 ♗xe7 ♕xe7 17 ♖ad1 a5 18 ♖xd8 ♕xd8 19 a3 and now:

a) Jansa-Poulsson, Oslo 1988 continued 19...a4?! (this looks like a mistake as the a-pawn becomes an additional weakness) 20 ♕e3 ♕a5 21 ♖d1 ♕b5 22 ♕c3 c5 23 ♖d6 ♗c6 24 ♗f1 ♕b6 25 ♕d2 h6 26 c3 ♕c7 27 ♗g2 ♗xg2 28 ♔xg2 ♘f8 29 ♕d3 g6 30 h5 c4 31 ♕e4 gxh5 32 ♕h7 ♖d8 33 ♖xe6 1-0.

b) Jansa-Paunovic, Namestovo 1987 went 19...♕c7 20 ♖d1 ♖d8 21 ♖xd8 ♕xd8 22 ♗e4 ♕c7 23 b4 axb4 24 axb4 and Black managed to survive another 23 moves of torture.

14 ♗g5 ♗b7

14...h6 15 ♗xe7 ♘xe7 16 ♕e3 b4 17 ♘a4 ♘d5 18 ♕d4 ♕a5 19 b3 gave White much the better game in Vasiukov-Damjanovic, Varna 1971. Adams' move is better, but White still maintains a useful space advantage because of his pawn on e5.

15 ♘e4 c5

And not 15...♕xe5? 16 ♘f6+.

16 ♘d6 ♖f8?!

A passive-looking move. Tiviakov suggested the immediate 16...♗xg5 17 hxg5 ♗c6, which saves several tempi on the game.

17 ♕g4 ♗xg5

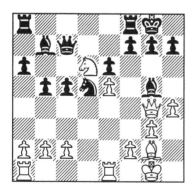

Adams must have been fully aware that opening the h-file is very dangerous, but he probably considered it the lesser evil. After 17...♗xd6 18 exd6

♕xd6 (18...♕d7 19 ♗xd5 ♗xd5 20 ♗f6 g6 21 ♕f4 and ♕h6 will be mate) 19 ♗h6 White wins the exchange, while 17...♔h8 18 ♗xe7 ♕xe7 19 c4! bxc4 20 ♕xc4 leaves the c5-pawn indefensible.

18 hxg5 ♗c6 19 ♗e4 ♘e7 20 ♖ad1 ♗xe4?!

With White's bishop pointing at the h7-square this is an understandable reaction. But 20...♖ad8 would have been more precise.

21 ♕xe4 ♖ab8?!

Black should still put the rook on the d-file. White uses the time he's being given to edge forward on the kingside.

22 f4 ♖fd8 23 ♔f2 c4 24 g4! ♖d7 25 ♖h1! ♘g6 26 ♔g3 ♕c5 27 c3 f6

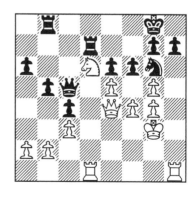

A despairing attempt to break

White's stranglehold, but it drops the exchange. After 27...♕c7 or 27...♘f8 White could increase the pressure by doubling rooks on the d-file.

28 gxf6 gxf6 29 ♘e8! ♖xe8 30 ♖xd7 fxe5 31 f5!

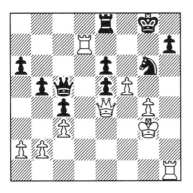

Not giving Black any chances.

31...♖f8 32 ♖dxh7 exf5 33 gxf5 ♘f4 34 ♖h8+ ♔f7 35 ♕b7+ ♔f6 36 ♖1h6+ ♔xf5 37 ♕h7+ 1-0

Game 26
Volzhin-Reefat
Dhaka 2001

---

1 e4 c5 2 ♘f3 ♘c6 3 d4 cxd4 4 ♘xd4 ♕c7 5 ♘c3 e6 6 g3 a6 7 ♗g2 ♘f6 8 0-0 ♗c5

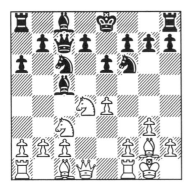

9 ♘xc6 dxc6 10 ♘a4 ♗a7

Black's other move is 10...♗e7 but Volzhin has had some success here too after 11 e5, for example 11...♘d7 (and not 11...♕xe5 12 ♘b6 ♖b8 13 ♗f4 etc.) 12 ♖e1 0-0 (after 12...♘xe5 13 ♗f4 ♗d6 14 ♕d4 c5 15 ♘xc5 ♗xc5 16 ♕xe5 ♕xe5 17 ♗xe5 White gets the better endgame due to his queenside majority and strong bishop on g2) 13 ♗f4 ♖d8 (13...b5 14 ♘c3 ♗b4 15 ♕g4 ♗xc3 16 bxc3 ♔h8 17 ♕h5 was also good for White in Popovic-Gross, Melk 1999) 14 ♘c3! ♘f8 15 ♕h5 ♘g6 16 ♘e4 ♘xf4 (16...♗d7 17 ♗g5 ♕xe5 18 ♘f6+ gxf6 19 ♖xe5 left Black with inadequate compensation for the queen in Volzhin-Lindberg, Stockholm 2002) 17 gxf4 ♖f8 18 ♖ad1 ♗d7 19 ♘f6+ gxf6 20 ♖e3 1-0 Volzhin-Tunik, Russia 2000.

11 c4 ♘d7 12 b4!?

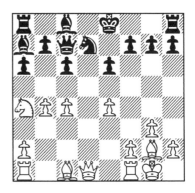

A very interesting possibility that casts doubt on Black's set up. The idea is to shut Black's bishop on a7 out of play with c4-c5, a plan that Reefat resists energetically. In an earlier game, Popovic-Miladinovic, Novi Sad 1984, White played 12 ♕g4 but after 12...♗d4 13 ♗f4 ♕a5 the position was just a mess.

12...b5 13 ♘b2 c5!?

A radical way of preventing c4-c5, but Black runs into an irritating pin on the c-file.

14 bxc5 0-0 15 cxb5 axb5 16 ♗e3 ♘xc5 17 ♖c1 ♕e7

This runs into trouble, but it's difficult to see a good alternative.

18 e5 ♘b7

After 18...♖b8 White plays 19 ♕d6!.

19 ♖e1 ♗xe3 20 ♖xe3 b4

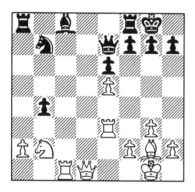

Preventing White from doubling on the c-file but giving him a4 for his knight. 20...♖xa2 is met by 21 ♕b3 ♖a8 22 ♖ec3! ♖b8 23 ♖c7 ♘a5 (23...♕g5 24 ♕xb5) 24 ♕c3 b4 25 ♕d4 ♕e8 26 ♕a7 etc.

21 ♘a4! ♖a5 22 ♘b6 ♘c5 23 ♕d6 ♕xd6 24 exd6 ♗d7 25 ♗f1 1-0

This quiet bishop move cuts out any checks on the 8th rank. After 25 ♗f1 ♖b8 there is 26 ♖xc5 ♖xc5 27 ♘xd7 as now Black cannot escape with 27...♖c1.

Game 27
Timman-Romanishin
Sarajevo 1984

---

1 e4 c5 2 ♘f3 e6 3 d4 cxd4 4 ♘xd4 ♘c6 5 ♘c3 a6 6 g3 ♘ge7

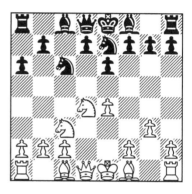

Taimanov's manoeuvre, which intends to simplify the position with 7...♘xd4 followed by 8...♘c6. By retreating his knight from d4 White can ask why Black's knight has gone to e7, so why does Black not capture on d4 immediately? The answer is that after 6...♘xd4 7 ♕xd4 ♘e7 White can emphasise the weakness of the d6-square with 8 ♗f4!, for example:

a) 8...♘g6 9 ♗d6 ♗xd6 10 ♕xd6 ♕e7 11 ♕b6 ♕d8 12 ♘a4 ♕xb6 13 ♘xb6 ♖b8 14 0-0-0 was awkward for Black in Kholmov-Karpov, Riga 1970.

b) 8...♘c6 9 ♕d2 f6 10 ♗d6 ♗xd6 11 ♕xd6 ♕e7 12 ♕d2 b5 13 0-0-0 ♘e5 14 f4 ♘f7 15 ♗g2 ♖a7 16 ♖he1 0-0 17 ♖e3 ♖c7 18 ♖d3 and Black was under pressure in Ciric-Krnic, Yugoslavia 1982.

7 ♘b3

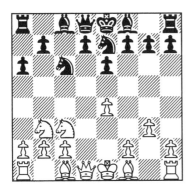

7...d6

Black must decide how to complete his development and this envisages the elaborate plan of bringing the knight round to b6 via c8. He has tried several alternatives:

a) 7...♘g6 does not make much sense in this position as the knight has very few prospects on this square. Short-Holm, Plovdiv 1983 continued 8 ♗g2 b5 9 0-0 ♗e7 10 ♘d5!? ♗b7 (or 10...exd5 11 exd5 ♗b7 12 dxc6 ♗xc6 13 ♗xc6 dxc6 14 ♕f3 with strong pressure) 11 ♘xe7 ♕xe7 12 a4 b4 13 a5 0-0 14 ♗e3 d6 15 ♖e1 ♘ge5 16 ♕e2 and White was clearly on top here because of his bishop pair and better pawn structure.

b) 7...b5 8 ♗g2 d6 (and not 8...♗b7 because of 9 ♘c5) 9 0-0 ♗b7 (9...♖b8 10 ♗e3 g6 11 f4 ♗g7 was Estrin-Taimanov, Albania 1974 and now 12 ♕d2 ♖b7 13 ♖ad1 ♖d7 14 f5! would have given White a very strong attack) 10 a4 b4 11 ♘a2 ♘c8 12 ♗d2 a5 13 c3 gave White some pressure in Vogt-Moor, Lenk 2002.

c) 7...♘a5 is strongly met by the reply 8 ♕h5!

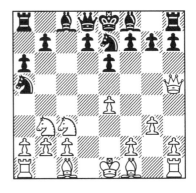

and now:

c1) 8...b5 9 ♘xa5 ♕xa5 10 ♗g2 ♗b7 11 0-0 ♘c6 12 ♗f4 ♗e7 13 ♘d5 exd5 14 exd5 0-0 15 dxc6 ♗xc6 16 c3 left White with a solid positional plus in Timman-Andersson, Holland 1978.

c2) 8...♘ec6 9 ♗g5!? ♕c7 10 ♗f4!? d6 11 ♘xa5 ♘xa5 12 0-0-0 ♘c6 (and not 12...♗d7 13 e5! d5 14 ♘xd5! exd5 15 e6 etc.) 13 ♕c5! dxc5 14 ♗xc7 and White had a clear plus in the endgame in Timman-Andersson, Holland 1978.

8 ♗g2 ♗d7 9 0-0 ♘c8 10 a4 ♗e7 11 ♕e2 0-0 12 ♗e3 ♕c7 13 f4 ♗f6 14 ♖fd1 ♖b8

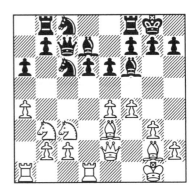

Black's position seems solid enough but he is badly in need of some counterplay. After White's reply, Black's last move fails miserably on this score.

14...♞a5? is bad because of 15 ♞xa5 ♛xa5 16 e5, while 14...b6 does not look much better after 15 ♛c4 threatening 16 e5. Black should probably play 14...♝xc3 but after 15 bxc3 he still needs a decent plan.

15 a5! ♜d8 16 ♞a4! ♞6e7

With White's knight en route for b6, Black is already in a very bad way. If he had snatched the a5-pawn with 16...♞xa5 there would have followed 17 ♞xa5 ♛xa5 18 e5 ♝e7 (18...dxe5 19 ♞b6 wins immediately) 19 ♞b6 ♛b5 (19...♛b4 20 c3 ♛b5 21 c4 transposes) 20 c4 ♛b4 21 exd6 ♝f6 (Black loses a piece after either 21...♝xd6? 22 ♞xd7 ♜xd7 23 c5 or 21...♞xb6? 22 dxe7 ♜e8 23 ♛f2) 22 ♞xd7 ♜xd7 23 c5 with a huge advantage for White.

17 c3

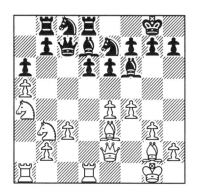

17...e5?!

17...g6 was probably better, but in any case Black's position is hardly enviable.

18 f5 b5

In this position 18...b6 would have been preferable as after 19 ♞xb6 Black can play 19...♞xb6 20 axb6 ♜xb6. Then 21 ♝xb6? ♛xb6+ wins the knight on

b3, so White's best is 21 ♜a3 with pressure against the a6-pawn.

19 ♞b6! h6 20 h4 b4 21 c4!

Maintaining a mighty grip is better than either 21 cxb4 or 21 ♛xa6.

21...♝e8 22 ♛f2 h5 23 ♛f3?!

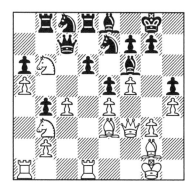

Giving Black something to play for with the following exchange sacrifice. 23 ♝f3 is simpler as 23...g6 is answered by 24 fxg6 fxg6 25 ♝xh5 etc.

23...♞xb6! 24 ♝xb6 ♜xb6 25 axb6 ♛xb6+ 26 ♛f2

After 26 ♔h2 Black gets some counterplay with 26...♞c6 27 ♛xh5 ♞d4 28 ♞xd4 exd4, intending 29...♝e5.

26...♛c7 27 c5 ♝b5

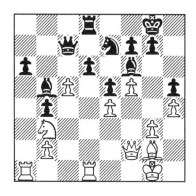

28 ♜ac1

The rook may be better placed where

it is. 28 cxd6 ♖xd6 29 ♖xd6 ♕xd6 30 ♗f1 is simpler.

28...♘c6 29 cxd6 ♖xd6 30 ♖d5 ♕d8! 31 ♕d2 ♘d4 32 ♘xd4 ♖xd5 33 exd5 exd4 34 ♕xb4 d3

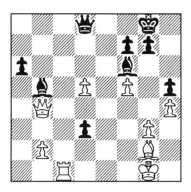

After staging a remarkable fight-back, Romanishin makes a fatal slip. The better 34...♗e5 would have left matters far from clear.

35 ♗f3 ♗e5 36 ♔g2 ♕f6 37 ♗xh5 ♕xf5 38 ♕g4 ♕f6

38...♕xg4 39 ♗xg4 ♗xb2 was a better try, but probably still lost for Black after 40 ♖d1.

39 ♖f1 ♕h6 40 ♗xf7+ 1-0

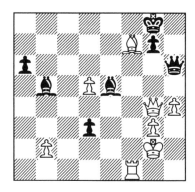

Summary

The theoretically approved play of Adams-Anand is worse for Black but seems tenable with accurate play. The same can be said of 8...♗e7 and 9...0-0, though once again he has a tough struggle for just half-a-point. Volzhin-Reefat spells serious trouble for 8...♗c5.

Black can certainly get a more fighting game with 8...h6 or 6...♘ge7, but White's chances certainly look preferable here. Frankly, I think Black may do better to transpose into a Scheveningen by playing 6...d6.

CHAPTER FIVE

The Kan Variation

A close relative of the Paulsen, the Kan Variation (1 e4 c5 2 ♘f3 e6 3 ♘c3 a6 4 d4 cxd4 5 ♘xd4) can easily transpose into lines we have just covered. The focus in this chapter is on the pure Kan lines in which Black delays or avoids ...♘b8-c6.

Black's sharpest and most logical line is to play 5...b5,

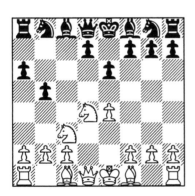

after which 6 g3 ♗b7 7 ♗g2 0-0 8 0-0, as in Game 28, is critical. If Black knows what he's doing he can snatch the e4-pawn and bail out into a reasonable endgame, though here too White keeps some initiative. Tseitlin-Kobalija

(Game 29) serves as a warning about the ineffectiveness of 8 ♗g5 (or 8 ♕e2 as given in the notes), which does not fit in with White's set-up at all. Playing White against the Sicilian calls for bold and sharp play.

In Nunn-Sigurjonsson (Game 30) Black precedes ...b7-b5 with ...♕c7, which gives White time to develop and play 9 ♖e1. Black's prospects look much worse here than in Game 28 because the e-pawn is defended and White can start operating with a2-a4.

The 6...♗b4 of Movsesian-Bezold (Game 31) is a very reasonable line for Black. After White retreats his knight from d4 (7 ♘de2) Black opts for a kind of Scheveningen set-up. Although White's space gives him the more comfortable game, Black has fighting chances in the complex middlegame.

Game 28
Guliev-Prasad
Abudhabi 1999

---

1 e4 c5 2 ♘f3 e6 3 d4 cxd4 4 ♘xd4

a6 5 ♘c3 b5 6 g3 ♗b7

For 6...♕c7 see Game 30.

7 ♗g2 ♘f6 8 0-0!?

For 8 ♗g5 and 8 ♕e2 see Game 29.

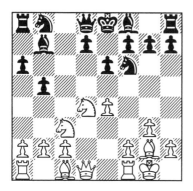

8...b4 9 ♘a4 ♗xe4

The alternative way to capture is with 9...♘xe4, after which White obtains strong pressure with 10 ♖e1 d5 11 c4 (and not 11 ♘xe6? fxe6 12 ♕h5+ g6 13 ♕e5 because of 13...♕d7 14 ♕xh8 ♕xa4, all of which happened in Enjuto Velasco-V.Georgiev, Madrid 2001) 11...bxc3 12 bxc3 ♗d6 13 ♖b1 ♕c7 14 ♕b3 ♖a7 15 ♗e3 ♗c8 16 c4 as in Barczay-Votava, Budapest 1995.

10 ♗xe4 ♘xe4 11 ♖e1

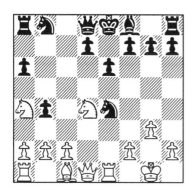

11...d5

After 11...♘c5 there follows 12 ♕f3

♖a7 13 ♘xc5 ♗xc5 14 ♘b3 d6 (14...♗e7 15 ♗e3 ♖c7 16 ♗b6 wins the exchange) 15 ♕h5 0-0 (the most dangerous threat was 16 ♖xe6+) 16 ♘xc5 dxc5 17 ♕xc5 ♖c7 18 ♕xb4 ♖xc2 19 ♕b3 ♖c5 20 ♗e3 ♖b5 21 ♕c3 and with the bishop pair and a queenside pawn majority, White was clearly better in Antal-Szieberth, Budapest 2000.

12 ♘xe6!?

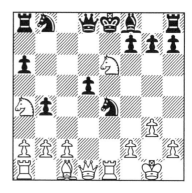

Once White knows this is playable it must be difficult to resist. A less spectacular try is 12 c4, though Black can defend with 12...bxc3 13 ♘xc3 ♘xc3 14 bxc3 ♗c5 (14...♗e7 15 ♖xe6 0-0 is also possible as in Asauskas-Kveinys, Vilnius 2002) 15 ♕g4 ♗xd4 16 cxd4 0-0 17 ♗g5 f5 18 ♕f4 ♕d7 19 ♖ac1 ♘c6, when White's compensation was unconvincing in Rausis-Marciano, Paris 1995.

12...fxe6 13 ♕h5+ g6

Bogdan Lalic prepared this as White against me in one of the Southend (Redbus) 2000 ten-minute play-off games. Not knowing what had hit me, I played 13...♔d7? and was butchered after 14 ♖xe4 dxe4 15 ♗f4 ♔c6 16 ♖d1 ♘d7 17 ♕e2 e5 18 ♕xe4+ ♔c7 19 ♕c4+ ♔b7 20 ♕d5+ 1-0. The text is much better as Black gets to exchange queens into an equal-looking endgame.

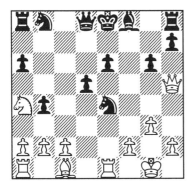

14 ♕e5 ♕f6 15 ♖xe4 ♕xe5 16 ♖xe5 ♔f7

Defending e6 and preparing to develop the rest of his pieces. At this point the position looks fine for Black.

17 ♖e2

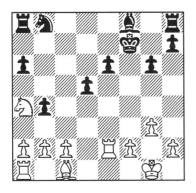

I don't think this is the most awkward move for Black. In the game Antal-Szilagyi, Balatonlelle 2000 White played 17 ♖e3!, after which 17...♘d7 (Black can also play 17...♘c6) 18 ♗d2 a5 19 ♖f3+ ♔g7 20 ♖e1 ♖a6 21 ♗f4 ♗e7 22 ♖d3 ♗f6 23 c4 d4?! left Black somewhat worse due to his 'bad' bishop and White's passed c-pawn. Instead, 23...bxc3 with approximate equality is

better.

17...♘c6

Black can also play 17...♘d7, for example:

a) 18 a3 a5 19 b3 ♗e7 20 ♗b2 ♖hc8 was already slightly better for Black in Bobras-Chuchelov, Cappelle la Grande 2002.

b) 18 ♗e3 ♗g7 19 ♖d1 ♖hc8 20 ♖d3 a5 21 a3 ♖a6 22 axb4 axb4 23 b3 ♘e5 24 ♖d1 and now 24...♖ac6 won the c-pawn in Brynell-C.Hansen, Reykjavik 2000.

18 ♗e3 ♗g7 19 ♗c5 ♖he8 20 a3 a5 21 ♔g2 ♖ac8 22 ♖d1 bxa3 23 bxa3 ♖b8 24 ♘b6 ♖b7

This looks rather cumbersome and passive. A much crisper and simpler move was 24...♗f8, after which 25 ♗xf8 (or 25 ♘d7 ♗xc5 26 ♘xc5 ♖b5) 25...♖xb6 is if anything better for Black.
25 ♖d3 ♗f6 26 ♖f3! ♖eb8 27 g4 g5 28 ♘a4 e5 29 ♘c3 ♔e6 30 ♖d2 d4 31 ♘e4 ♖f7 32 c3 h6 33 ♖e2 ♗g7 34 ♖d3 ♔d5 35 f3 ♖f4 36 cxd4 exd4 37 ♖c2 ♗e5 38 ♗f8 fxf8 39 ♖c5+ ♔e6 40 ♖xc6+ ♔d7 41 ♖c2 ♖fc8 42 ♖e2 ♗g7 43 h4 gxh4 44 f4 a4 45 f5 ♖b3 46 f6 ♖xd3 47 fxg7 ♖e3 48 ♘f6+ ♔e7 49 ♖f2 ♖g3+ 50

♔h2 ♚f7??

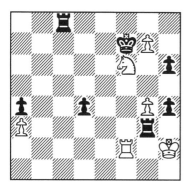

Even now Black would have been okay after 50...♚e6 51 g8♕+ ♖xg8 52 ♘xg8 ♖xg4 53 ♘xh6 ♖g3.

51 ♘e8+! 1-0

A nasty surprise. It's curtains after 51...♚xe8 (or 51...♚g8 52 ♖f8+) 52 ♖f8+ ♚d7 53 ♖xc8.

Game 29
Ma.Tseitlin-Kobalija
Bugojno 1999

---

1 e4 c5 2 ♘f3 e6 3 ♘c3 a6 4 g3 b5 5 d4 cxd4 6 ♘xd4 ♗b7 7 ♗g2 ♘f6 8 ♗g5

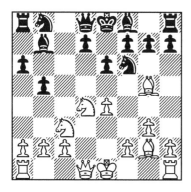

This move has appeared quite frequently in practice, but is less than

harmless for Black. The best alternative to 8 0-0 is 8 ♕e2, after which Black has a number of reasonable ways to play it.

a) 8...♕b6 9 ♗e3 ♗c5 10 0-0-0 ♘c6 11 ♘xc6 ♗xc6 12 ♗xc5 ♕xc5 13 f4 ♖c8 14 ♚b1 b4 15 ♘d5 ♗xd5 16 exd5 0-0 17 dxe6 dxe6 was nice for Black in Smirin-Markowski, Moscow 2002.

b) 8...♘c6 9 ♘xc6 ♗xc6 10 0-0 (10 ♘d5 is ineffective after 10...♖c8) 10...b4 11 e5 ♗xg2 12 ♚xg2 bxc3 13 exf6 ♕xf6 14 ♕e4 ♕d8 15 bxc3 ♗e7 was approximately equal in de la Villa Garcia-Strikovic, San Sebastian 1994.

c) 8...b4 9 ♘a4 ♕a5 (opening the position with 9...d5 may also be playable, but looks more risky) 10 b3 ♘c6 11 ♗e3 ♘xd4 12 ♗xd4 ♕b5 13 ♕d3 ♗e7 14 0-0 e5 15 ♗e3 d5 and Black had a fully equal game in Hellers-Kengis, Denmark 1997.

8...♗e7 9 0-0 b4 10 ♘a4 ♕a5 11 ♗xf6 ♗xf6 12 ♘b3

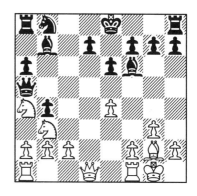

12...♕c7

This solid move gives Black a nice game, but it is not the most incisive line. After 12...♕xa4 13 ♘c5 ♕c6 14 ♘xb7 Black can play 14...♗e5! and obtain more than enough compensation for the exchange after 15 ♘d6+ ♕xd6 16

♕xd6 ♗xd6 17 e5 ♗xe5 18 ♗xa8 ♗xb2 19 ♖ab1 ♗c3 20 a3 a5 21 axb4 axb4. Bistric-Sax, Sarajevo 1982 and Benjamin-Serper, Salt Lake City 1999 continued 22 ♗e4 ♔e7, with White getting tortured on both occasions.

13 ♘ac5 ♗c6

Black is slightly better because of his two bishops. It needs some good play by Tseitlin to keep them at bay.

14 ♘d3 a5 15 a3 bxa3 16 ♖xa3 a4

Black might have been better off had he found a way to avoid this. Now White gets the b4-square for a knight.

17 ♘d2 0-0 18 ♖e1 d6 19 c3 ♖a7 20 ♘b4 ♗d7 21 ♗f1 ♖d8 22 ♘f3 ♗e8 23 ♘d4 ♕b6 24 ♘dc2 ♘d7 25 ♘e3 ♘c5 26 ♗g2

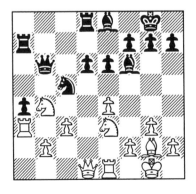

White's position is rock solid and there is no way to make further progress for Black. He keeps trying for a while, though.

26...♕b8 27 h4 h6 28 ♕f3 ♗e7 29 ♘ec2 ♕c7 30 ♕e3 ♕b6 31 ♘d4 ♖c7 32 ♖aa1 ♖cc8 33 ♖ed1 ♗f6 34 ♘dc2 ♕b8 35 ♖a3 ♗b5 36 ♘d4 ♗e8 37 ♗f1 ♕b6 38 ♘dc2 ♖b8 39 ♖aa1 ♕b7 40 ♖e1 ♖bc8 41 ♘a3 ♕b8 42 ♖ad1 ♘b3 43 ♘a6 ♕b7 44 ♘b4 ♕b8 45 ♘a6 ♕a8 46 ♘b4 ♕b8 47 ♘a6 ½-½

> ## Game 30
> **Nunn-Sigurjonsson**
> London 1975

1 e4 c5 2 ♘f3 e6 3 d4 cxd4 4 ♘xd4 a6 5 ♘c3 ♕c7 6 g3 b5

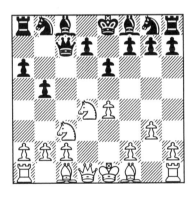

For 6...♗b4 see Game 31.

7 ♗g2 ♗b7 8 0-0 d6

After 8...♘c6 9 ♖e1 Black is in serious danger of being hit by ♘c3-d5, for example 9...d6 (Black should play 9...♘e5, after which 10 ♗f4 d6 11 a4 bxa4 12 ♘xa4 ♘f6 13 b3 ♗e7 14 ♗c1 0-0 15 c4 was worse for him but playable in Kudrin-Quinteros, New York 1983) 10 a4 b4 11 ♘d5!

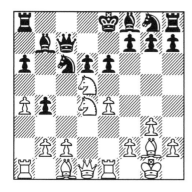

11...♕a5 12 ♕h5!? (the less spectacular 12 ♘xc6 ♗xc6 13 c3 bxc3 14 b4 was also very good for White in Hulak-Sinclair, Graz 1972) 12...exd5 13 ♘xc6 ♗xc6 14 exd5+ ♘e7 15 ♗g5 ♗d7 16 ♗xe7 ♗xe7 17 ♕g5 ♕d8 18 ♕xg7 ♖f8 19 ♕xh7 ♗c8 20 ♖e4 and White went on to win in the game I.Almasi-Bardosi, Hungarian Team Championship 1992.

Taimanov's suggestion of 8...♗c5 9 ♘b3 ♗e7 was tried in Huguet-Panno, Las Palmas 1973, after which I suggest 10 ♖e1 (10 ♗f4 d6 11 ♕e2 ♘c6 12 ♖ad1 ♘f6 proved ineffective in the game) 10...d6 11 a4, for example 11...b4 12 ♘a2 ♘c6 13 ♗d2 a5 14 c3 bxc3 15 ♘xc3 ♘f6 16 ♘b5 ♕d7 17 ♗f4 with strong pressure.

9 ♖e1 ♗e7

After 9...♘d7 there follows 10 a4 b4 (after 10...bxa4 11 ♖xa4 ♘gf6 the move 12 ♘d5 is strong) 11 ♘a2! (11 ♘d5 is interesting but far from clear whereas the text is simple and strong) 11...a5 12 c3 bxc3 13 ♘xc3 ♘gf6 14 ♘cb5 ♕b8 15 ♗g5 ♘c5 (after 15...♗e7 there is 16 ♖c1, threatening 17 ♘c7) 16 e5! ♗xg2 (or 16...dxe5 17 ♘c6 etc.) 17 exf6 ♗e4 and 18 ♖c1 gave White a strong attack in Kupreichik-A.Petrosian, Lvov 1988.

10 a4 bxa4

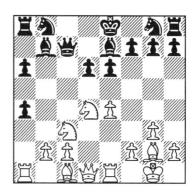

Here too the move 10...b4 is well met by 11 ♘a2, after which 11...♘f6 12 ♗d2 a5 13 ♘b5 ♕c6 14 c3 bxc3 15 ♗xc3 leaves Black with serious problems

11 ♕h5! g6

White was threatening 12 ♘xe6. This would also be the answer to 11...♘f6.

12 ♕e2 ♘c6 13 ♖xa4 ♘xd4 14 ♖xd4 ♖c8 15 ♗d2 ♘f6?!

After White's reply Black can no longer castle. A better try would have been 15...♗f6!? 16 ♖b4 ♗g7, intending ...♘e7 and ...0-0.

16 ♗h6! ♕b6 17 ♖d3 ♖c7

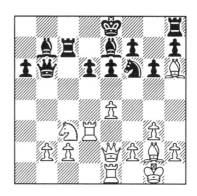

And not 17...♕xb2 18 ♖b1, skewering the queen against the bishop on b7.

18 e5! dxe5 19 ♗xb7 ♖xb7

Or if 19...♕xb7 there follows 20 ♕xe5 ♖c5 21 ♕d4, once again leaving Black in a straight jacket.

20 ♕xe5 ♕c7

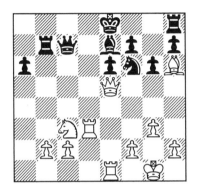

This loses the exchange, but it's difficult to see a move for Black. Perhaps 20...♖g8 is the only move to keep the game going.

21 ♕xc7 ♖xc7 22 ♗g7 ♖g8 23 ♗xf6 ♗xf6 24 ♘d5 ♗d8 25 ♘xc7+ ♗xc7 26 ♖ed1 1-0

Game 31
Movsesian-Bezold
Bad Homburg 1996

---

1 e4 c5 2 ♘f3 e6 3 ♘c3 a6 4 d4 cxd4 5 ♘xd4 ♕c7 6 g3 ♗b4

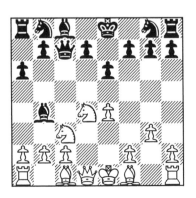

7 ♘de2

The knight is quite well placed here and White may later play g3-g4 and bring it to the g3-square. The alternative is 7 ♗d2, after which Shabalov-S.Salov, Hamburg 1999 continued 7...♘f6 8 ♗g2 ♗e7 9 f4 (9 0-0 d6 10 ♗e3 transposes to Game 17) 9...d6 10 g4 ♘c6 11 ♘b3 b5 12 g5 ♘d7 13 ♕h5 and now Fedorowicz suggested the immediate 13...♘b6 with good counterplay (in the game Black played 13...g6?!, which weakened his kingside prematurely).

7...♘f6 8 ♗g2 ♗e7 9 0-0 0-0 10 h3

An interesting alternative is to play 10 b3 followed by ♗b2 with very harmonious development.

10...♘c6 11 f4 d6

Black should play 11...b5 12 ♗e3 ♗b7 13 g4 d5 as in Tarjan-Gheorghiu, Los Angeles 1974, when according to Gheorghiu White's best was 14 exd5 (in the game he played 14 e5) 14...♖ad8 15 g5 ♘xd5 16 ♘xd5 exd5 17 ♘d4 with what looks like a slight edge.

12 g4 ♖e8?!

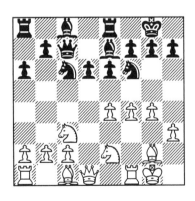

Somewhat passive. The attempt to break out with 12...d5 13 exd5 ♖d8 is met by 14 f5! exf5 (or 14...exd5 15 ♘f4!) 15 gxf5 ♘b4 16 ♗e3 ♕d6 17 ♘f4, when

White was a good pawn up in Ciric-Miles, Dortmund 1976.

In Motwani-Panno, Dubai Olympiad 1986 Black played 12...b5 and after 13 a3 ♖b8 14 g5 ♘d7 15 f5 (the more patient 15 h4 seems better to me) Panno recommended 15...♖e8, intending ...♘de5.

13 g5 ♘d7 14 h4 ♗f8 15 h5 g6 16 hxg6 hxg6 17 f5 ♘de5 18 ♘f4 b5 19 ♘cd5! exd5 20 ♘xd5 ♕d8 21 ♘f6+ ♔g7 22 ♗e3 ♗e7

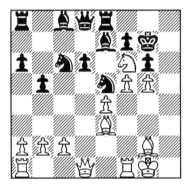

Giving up some material to bail himself out of a mating attack. 22...♖e7 is met by 23 ♕e1 followed by 24 ♕h4.

23 ♘xe8+ ♕xe8 24 f6+ ♔g8 25 fxe7 ♕xe7

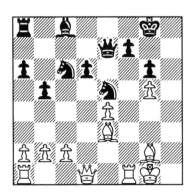

With the extra exchange White must

be winning. But Bezold puts up tough resistance, with his knight on e5 holding things together.

26 ♕e2 a5 27 ♖f4 ♕xg5 28 ♖xf7 ♕d8 29 ♖f4 ♗e6 30 ♖af1 ♕e7 31 ♕f2 ♖c8 32 ♕g3 ♘d8 33 c3 ♘df7 34 ♗d4

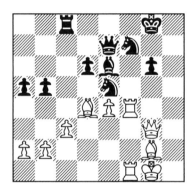

An excellent post for the bishop. Even so the game doesn't win itself and White decides he has to sacrifice the exchange in order to engineer a combinative breakthrough.

34...♗xa2 35 ♖f6 ♗e6 36 ♖xg6+! ♘xg6 37 ♕xg6+ ♔f8 38 ♖f6 ♗c4 39 ♖f5 ♔e8 40 ♗f6 ♕c7 41 ♗d4 ♕e7 42 ♖f6 ♖b8 43 b3! ♗xb3 44 e5! ♔d7

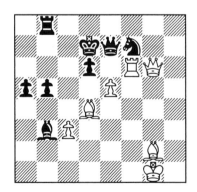

The point behind White's 43rd move

is that after 44...dxe5 45 ♕g8+ ♔d7 (45...♕f8 46 ♗c6+ ♔e7 47 ♗c5+) 46 ♕xb8 ♕xf6 47 ♕b7+ ♔e8 there is 48 ♕xb5+ ♔f8 49 ♗c5+ ♔g7 50 ♕xb3 picking up the bishop.

45 e6+ ♗xe6 46 ♗h3! ♘h8 47 ♗xe6+ ♕xe6 48 ♕g7+ ♕e7 49 ♖xd6+ ♔xd6 50 ♗c5+

50...♔xc5

At first sight this looks as if it should be a draw, but Movsesian has calculated that he will also win Black's queenside pawns because his rook and knight are loose.

51 ♕xe7+ ♔c6 52 ♕e6+ ♔c7 53 ♕e5+ ♔b7 54 ♕xb5+ ♔c7 55 ♕xa5+ ♔b7 56 ♕b5+ ♔c7 57 ♕e5+ ♔b7 58 ♕g7+ ♔c6 59 ♔f2 ♖e8 60 c4 ♔d6 61 c5+ ♔e6 62 ♕g4+ ♔f6 63 ♕d4+ ♔f7 64 ♕d7+ ♔f8 65 c6 ♘g6 66 ♕f5+ ♔g7 67 c7 ♘e7 68 ♕e6 ♔f8 69 ♕f6+ ♔g8 70 ♕xe7!

♖xe7 71 c8♕+ ♔g7 72 ♔f3 ♖f7+ 73 ♔g4 ♖f6 74 ♕c3 ♔g6 75 ♕d3+ ♔h6 76 ♕c2 ♖g6+ 77 ♔f5 ♔h7 78 ♕c3 ♖g7 79 ♔f6 ♔h8 80 ♕h3+ ♔g8 81 ♕h5 ♖c7 82 ♕d5+ ♔h7 83 ♕d3+ 1-0

83...♔g8 84 ♕d8+ wins the rook.

Summary

The sharpest line of the Kan involves an all-out attack on White's e4-pawn, though Black is in serious danger when he actually gets to take it. Game 28 should be studied quite carefully, especially the endgames with 17 ♖e3 that currently represent the last word. Black's other decent line was played in Game 31 and here White should play some practice games from the position after 12 g4. Experience is one of the best teachers.

CHAPTER SIX

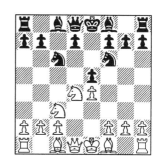

The Pelikan-Sveshnikov Variation

The Pelikan (1 e4 c5 2 ♘f3 ♘c6 3 d4 cxd4 4 ♘xd4 ♘f6 5 ♘c3 e5) together with the Sveshnikov sub-variation (6 ♘db5 d6 7 ♗g5 a6 8 ♘a3 b5!?) feature a very controversial form of ...e7-e5 Sicilian. For many years these lines were simply deemed to be bad for Black because White could play ♗c1-g5 and exchange a crucial defender of the d5-square. However, one fine day Bent Larsen tried the Pelikan (with 8...♗e6) in one game and showed that the position held many resources for Black. And players from Cheliabinsk, notably Evgeny Sveshnikov and Gennadi Timoshenko, started playing and winning with 8...b5.

Some years later White's sights had lowered considerably. Rather than expecting the d5-square to guarantee a full point from the outset, the battle was on to try and eke out at least some sort of advantage. Whilst this battle is still raging it would be inadvisable to join in; our objective is to find a good and economical line which has strategic similarities to the other variations in this book.

By keeping to a familiar pattern in which we understand the plans involved, we will play more effectively in the middlegame.

Against Sveshnikov's 8...b5,

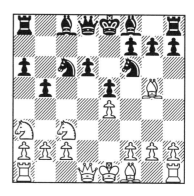

the line that fits the bill is 9 ♗xf6 gxf6 10 ♘d5 f5 11 c3 ♗g7 12 exf5 ♗xf5 13 ♘c2, after which White wants to strengthen his grip on the e4- and d5-squares with a kingside fianchetto. After 13...0-0 he should play 14 ♘ce3 ♗e6 15 g3 (as in the games Geller-Arakhamia, Shamkovich-Maguire and Adams-Salov – see Games 32-34), whilst 13...♗e6 should be met by the immediate 14 g3 (see Game 35). In any event, White has active and well-coordinated pieces that certainly make life difficult for Black. They can be devastating against anything but the most precise defence.

Of Black's other lines, Prasad-Koshy (Game 36) represents a simple and economical route to an advantage against 8...♗e6. With 6...h6 (Game 37) Black radically prevents ♗c1-g5 but White can obtain the two bishops and enjoy a clear edge in the endgame.

Game 32
Geller-Arakhamia
Aruba 1992

---

1 e4 c5 2 ♘f3 ♘c6 3 d4 cxd4 4 ♘xd4 ♘f6 5 ♘c3 e5 6 ♘db5 d6 7 ♗g5 a6 8 ♘a3 b5

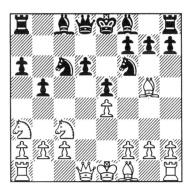

Sveshnikov's move, which essentially rehabilitated this opening from Black's point of view and turned it into a very fashionable defence.

9 ♗xf6 gxf6

Recapturing with the g-pawn gives Black a group of horrendous looking pawns on d6, e5, f6 and f7, but despite their weak appearance they may eventually start rolling forward. Black also has

the g-file and a potentially useful bishop pair. After 9...♕xf6 10 ♘d5 ♕d8 11 c3 White has a strong grip on d5 and Black has lost a lot of time.

10 ♘d5 f5

Black can also first play 10...♗g7 and, after 11 c3, play 11...f5. With the treatment I'm recommending for White this amounts to nothing more than a harmless transposition.

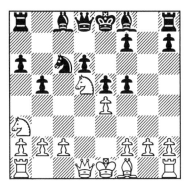

11 c3 ♗g7

If Black plays the greedy 11...fxe4 White has the powerful 12 ♗xb5 axb5 13 ♘xb5, for example 13...♕g5 (13...♗e6 is met by 14 ♘bc7+ ♔d7 15 ♘xa8 ♗xd5 16 ♕xd5 ♕xa8 17 ♕xe4 with a clear advantage) 14 ♘dc7+ (I prefer this to 14 ♘bc7+ ♔d8 15 ♘xa8 ♕xg2 16 ♖f1, which admittedly may also be good) 14...♔d8 15 ♕d5! ♗b7 16 ♕xf7 ♕e7 17 ♕f5 and White had a tremendous attack in the game Shamkovich-Wachtel, USA 1977. If White would prefer not to allow 11...fxe4, he could always play 11 exf5 ♗xf5 and then 12 c3.

12 exf5 ♗xf5 13 ♘c2 0-0 14 ♘ce3

Setting about establishing a grip on the d5-square which will also involve posting his bishop on g2. The immediate 14 g3?! is wrong because of 14...♗e4! 15 f3 ♗xd5 16 ♕xd5 ♘e7 followed by ...d6-d5.

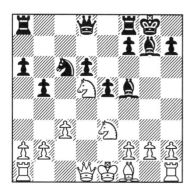

14...♗e6

Black has attempted to rehabilitate 14...♗g6 by meeting 15 h4 with 15...♗e4!? (if 15...f5 White can play 16 h5 ♗e8 17 g4! ♗d7 18 ♘xf5! ♗xf5 19 gxf5 with tremendous light square control; or if 15...h6 16 g4 with a bind) but a promising line for White is 16 ♗d3!? ♗xd5 17 ♘xd5 f5 18 ♕h5, after which 18...e4 19 ♗c2 ♔h8 (19...♘e5 may be better but this still looks promising for White after 20 0-0-0) 20 0-0-0 b4 21 g4! ♕e8 22 ♕xe8 ♖axe8 23 ♗a4 ♖c8 24 ♗xc6 ♖xc6 25 ♘xb4 left White a good pawn up in Velimirovic-Kapnisis, Athens 2000.

15 g3 b4

Trying to inflict some damage on White's structure. White cannot take this with his c-pawn as he needs to prevent Black's knight from landing on d4.

For 15...♖b8 see Game 33, while 15...♘e7 is featured in Game 34.

16 ♗g2 bxc3 17 bxc3 ♖c8 18 0-0 f5 19 ♕h5 ♔h8 20 ♖ad1 ♘e7 21 ♖d2

After 21 c4 Black would re-route his knight towards the d4-square with 21...♘c6 and obtain an excellent game.

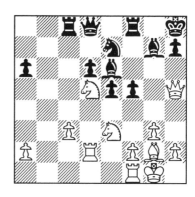

21...e4

Shutting the g2-bishop out of play. 21...♘xd5 22 ♘xd5 ♗xd5 23 ♖xd5 ♖xc3 24 ♖fd1 ♖c6 25 ♖xe5! wins back the pawn and leaves Black's position in ruins.

22 ♖fd1 ♗e5 23 ♘f4!?

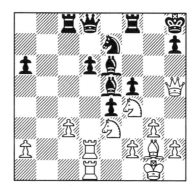

Initiating some dynamic play. After the standard 23 c4 Black plays 23...♘xd5 24 cxd5 ♗d7 with equality.

23...♗f7

After 23...♗xf4 24 gxf4 the d6-pawn is in trouble.

24 ♕h6 ♖c6 25 ♘e6 ♗xe6 26 ♕xe6 ♕e8 27 ♘c4

The tempting 27 ♘xf5? is bad because of 27...♖xf5 (27...♘xf5 28 ♕xe8 ♖xe8 29 ♗xe4 ♘e7 30 ♗xc6 ♘xc6 31 c4 followed by 32 f4 is winning) 28 ♗xe4 d5!, trapping the queen.

27...♖f6 28 ♘xd6 ♖xe6 29 ♘xe8 ♔g8 30 ♖d8 ♔f7 31 ♖1d7 ♖g6?

Having defended excellently up to this point, Black makes a fatal slip. After 31...♖xc3! 32 ♘d6+ ♔g6 33 ♗h3 ♖c6 Black is okay.

32 ♗f1 f4 33 ♗e2 f3 34 ♗d1!

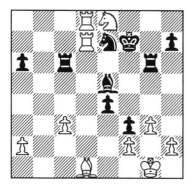

The deadly threat of 35 ♗b3+ costs Black the exchange and the game.

34...♖xc3 35 ♗b3+ ♖xb3 36 axb3 ♖b6 37 ♘d6+ ♗xd6 38 ♖xd6 ♖xb3 39 ♖d1 ♘f5 40 ♖8d2 ♖a3 41 ♖e1 h5 42 ♖dd1 ♖a4 43 ♖a1 ♖d4 44 ♖a5 ♔f6 45 ♖xa6+ ♘d6 46 h3 ♔g5 47 ♖a5+ ♔g6 48 ♖e5 ♖d2 49 h4 ♖d4 50 ♖g5+ ♔h6 51 ♖a1 ♖d2 52 ♖a8 ♔h7 53 ♖a7+ ♔h6 54 ♖e7 1-0

Game 33
Shamkovich-Maguire
Las Vegas 1994

---

1 e4 c5 2 ♘e2 ♘c6 3 d4 cxd4 4 ♘xd4 ♘f6 5 ♘c3 e5 6 ♘db5 d6 7 ♗g5 a6 8 ♗xf6 gxf6 9 ♘a3 b5 10 ♘d5 f5 11 c3 ♗g7 12 exf5 ♗xf5 13

♘c2 0-0 14 ♘ce3 ♗e6 15 g3 ♖b8

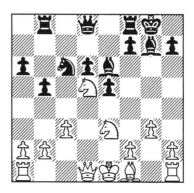

It is quite common for Black to evacuate the long diagonal, but this is probably just a waste of time.

16 ♗g2 f5 17 ♕h5 b4 18 0-0 bxc3 19 bxc3 ♕d7

This meets with an energetic response from Shamkovich. A better move may be 19...♘e7, after which White should occupy the b-file with 20 ♖ab1 with somewhat the better game (and not 20 ♖fd1 e4 21 ♖ac1 ♘xd5 22 ♘xd5 ♖b2!).

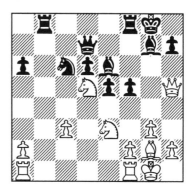

20 f4! ♕a7

The queen looks out of play on this square. 20...e4 is strongly met by 21 g4!, undermining Black's pawn chain, but 20...♖b5!? 21 ♖ad1 ♖c5 might have made more of a fight of it as the rook is quite effective here.

21 ♔h1 ♛c5 22 ♖ad1 ♖b2 23 fxe5! dxe5

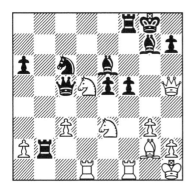

After 23...♘xe5 Shamkovich intended 24 ♘e7+ ♔h8 25 ♘7xf5 ♛xc3 26 ♘xg7 ♔xg7 27 ♖xf8 ♔xf8 28 ♖f1+ ♔g7, after which the sting in the tail is 29 ♘d1!.

24 ♖xf5!

And not 24 ♘xf5? ♖xg2!, which completely turns the tables.

24...♗xf5 25 ♘xf5 ♛f2 26 ♘de7+ ♘xe7 27 ♘xe7+ ♔h8 28 ♘g6+ ♔g8 29 ♗d5+ ♖f7 30 ♗xf7+ ♔xf7

Or if 30...♛xf7 then 31 ♖d8+ etc.

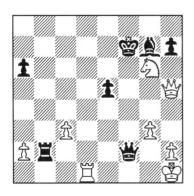

31 ♘xe5+

White could also play for mate with

31 ♖d7+ ♔g8 32 ♖d8+ ♔f7 33 ♘xe5+ and the decision not to do so was probably dictated by the ticking of the clock.

31...♔g8 32 ♛h3 ♖e2

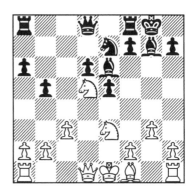

Or 32...♗xe5 33 ♛e6+ etc.

33 ♛e6+ ♔h8 34 ♘f7+ ♔g8 35 ♘h6+ 1-0

Game 34
Adams-Salov
Dortmund 1992

---

1 e4 c5 2 ♘f3 ♘c6 3 d4 cxd4 4 ♘xd4 ♘f6 5 ♘c3 e5 6 ♘db5 d6 7 ♗g5 a6 8 ♘a3 b5 9 ♗xf6 gxf6 10 ♘d5 ♗g7 11 c3 f5 12 exf5 ♗xf5 13 ♘c2 0-0 14 ♘ce3 ♗e6 15 g3 ♘e7

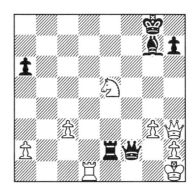

The exchange of all the minor pieces with this and a later ....♝h6 sets about making the weakness of d5 less important. There would simply be nothing left to land there.

16 ♗g2 ♖b8 17 0-0 ♘xd5 18 ♗xd5 ♔h8 19 a4 ♗h6!

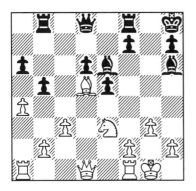

Intending to trade his bad bishop for White's good knight. Unfortunately for Salov, he does not follow up correctly.

20 axb5 axb5?

Black should take this opportunity to play 20...♗xe3, after which 21 fxe3 ♗xd5 22 ♕xd5 ♖xb5 23 ♕d2 a5 leaves him only slightly worse. He does not get a second chance to eliminate the knight.

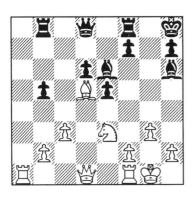

21 ♘c2! ♕d7 22 ♖a6 ♗h3 23 ♖e1 ♗g5 24 ♘b4 ♗d8 25 ♗e4 ♗b6 26

♘d5

A good alternative is 26 ♕h5, after which 26...f5 27 ♖xb6 fxe4 28 ♖xb8 ♖xb8 29 ♖xe4 leaves Black with a very ropy pawn structure.

26...f5 27 ♘xb6 ♕d8 28 ♘d7 ♕xd7 29 ♖xd6 ♕e7 30 ♖d7 ♕g5 31 ♗c2!

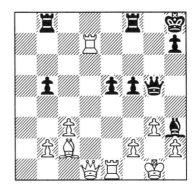

Getting ready to re-emerge via the b3-square.

31...e4?

Losing immediately. Black should play 31...♖be8, after which 32 f4! is strong but not necessarily the end for Black (less good is 32 ♕d6?! because of simply 32...♕f6).

32 ♕d4+ ♕f6 33 ♕a7 ♕h6 34 ♖a1 b4 35 ♕d4+ ♕f6 36 ♖aa7 ♕xd4 37 cxd4 1-0

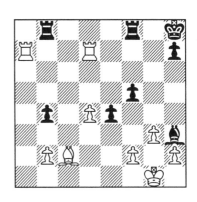

Game 35
A.Sokolov-Lastin
Russian Championship, Elista 1995

1 e4 c5 2 ♘f3 ♘c6 3 d4 cxd4 4 ♘xd4 ♘f6 5 ♘c3 e5 6 ♘db5 d6 7 ♗g5 a6 8 ♘a3 b5 9 ♗xf6 gxf6 10 ♘d5 f5 11 exf5 ♗xf5 12 c3 ♗g7 13 ♘c2 ♗e6!?

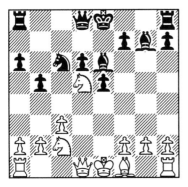

This move order was originally designed to avoid 13...0-0 14 ♘ce3 ♗e6 15 ♗d3, the point being that after 13...♗e6 14 ♘ce3 ♘e7 White cannot play 15 ♗d3 because it would lose a piece.

14 g3

A further point behind 13...♗e6 is that 14 ♘ce3 ♘e7 15 g3 ♘xd5 16 ♘xd5 0-0 leaves White with the wrong minor piece on d5. In the previous game we saw Adams taking the opportunity to recapture on d5 with the bishop.

14...0-0 15 ♗g2 ♖b8

The immediate 15...a5 may be more precise, not bothering to waste time with the rook. Topalov-Leko, Leon 1996 continued 16 0-0 f5 17 ♕e2! (in this position the queen's action on the e-file is not inhibited by the presence of a knight on e3, so this may well be more

promising than the standard 17 ♕h5, after which 17...b4 18 ♘ce3 ♔h8 19 ♖ad1 bxc3 20 bxc3 ♖b8 gives Black adequate counterplay) 17...♖b8 (17...b4 is strongly met by 18 ♘f4! as Black does not have the c4-square available to his bishop) 18 ♖fd1 ♔h8 (18...♕d7 19 ♖d2 ♕f7 20 ♖ad1 also looks good for White) 19 ♖d2 ♕d7 20 ♖ad1 ♕f7 (20...e4 is strongly met by 21 ♘f4! ♗e5 22 ♘xe6 ♕xe6 23 f4! exf3 24 ♗xf3 with much the better game) 21 b3 ♘a7 22 ♔h1 ♘c8 23 ♘a3 ♘a7 24 f4! ♗xd5 25 ♖xd5 exf4 26 gxf4 ♗xc3 27 ♕d3 ♗b2 28 ♘c2 and White's beautifully placed pieces were generating massive pressure.

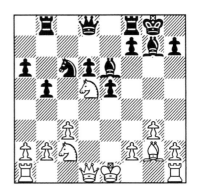

16 0-0 ♕d7

Ljubojevic-Illescas, Linares 1995 continued 16...a5 17 ♕h5 f5 18 ♖ad1 ♔h8 19 ♘ce3 ♘e7 and now Krasenkow claimed that 20 ♖d2 would have given White an edge.

17 a4!? a5

According to Nigel Short, 17...bxa4 18 ♖xa4 a5 19 ♘ce3!? ♖xb2 20 ♖c4 ♖c8 21 ♕h5 gives White a strong attack for the pawn, and with 22 f4 coming this looks very true.

Short-Kramnik, Novgorod 1995 featured 17...b4?! 18 ♘cxb4 ♘xb4 19 cxb4 ♗xd5 20 ♗xd5 ♖xb4 21 b3! and White was much better by virtue of his powerful bishop on d5.

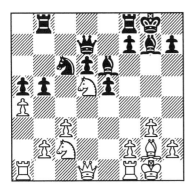

18 ♘ce3 ♔h8?!

18...b4!? would have been a better try. Now White takes the initiative and doesn't let go.

19 axb5 ♖xb5 20 ♕a4 ♖fb8

And not 20...♖xb2? because of 21 ♘c4 ♖b7 22 ♘db6 etc.

21 ♕h4! ♕d8

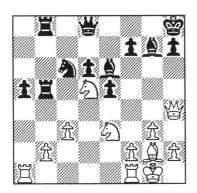

Attempting to bail out into and endgame, but there too Black is in trouble. After 21...♖xb2 there would follow 22 ♘f6! ♗xf6 23 ♕xf6+ ♔g8 24 ♖a4!, when 24...♕e7 25 ♕h6 ♘d8 26 ♘d5 wins on the spot.

22 ♕xd8+ ♘xd8 23 ♘c7 ♖xb2 24 ♘xe6 ♘xe6 25 ♘c4 ♖c2 26 ♘xd6 ♔g8

Letting the f7-pawn go with 26...♖xc3 is also miserable for Black after 27 ♘xf7+ ♔g8 28 ♘d6 ♖d3 29 ♘f5 ♖b5 30 ♖fc1 etc.

27 ♘e4 ♖b5 28 ♖fd1

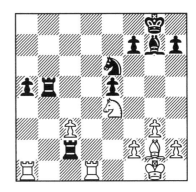

28...♔f8

Or if 28...♖bb2 there follows 29 ♗f1! ♖a2 30 ♗c4 ♖xa1 31 ♖xa1 followed by capturing the a-pawn and then ganging up on f7.

29 ♗f1 ♖b7

29...♖bb2 30 ♗d3 wins the exchange.

30 ♖xa5 ♔e7 31 ♘d6 ♖c7 32 ♘f5+ ♔f6 33 ♘e3 ♖2xc3 34 ♘d5+

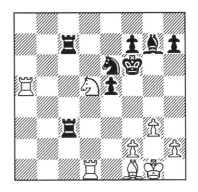

Winning the exchange and the game.

34...♔g6 35 ♘xc3 ♖xc3 36 ♖a6 ♗f8 37 ♗h3! ♔f6 38 ♗xe6 fxe6 39 ♖a7 h6 40 ♖dd7 ♗c5 41 ♖f7+ ♔g6 42 ♖g7+ ♔f5 43 ♖af7+ ♔e4 44 ♖g6 1-0

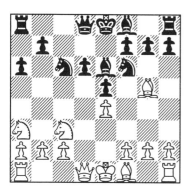

Game 36
Prasad-Koshy
Madras 1995

1 e4 c5 2 ♘f3 ♘c6 3 d4 cxd4 4 ♘xd4 ♘f6 5 ♘c3 e5 6 ♘db5 d6 7 ♗g5 a6 8 ♘a3 ♗e6

This is the main alternative to Sveshnikov's 8...b5 and probably the only really playable alternative. Other moves seem rather dubious, for example:

a) 8...♗e7 9 ♘c4 ♘d4 (9...♗e6 10 ♗xf6 gxf6 11 ♘e3 ♕d7 12 ♘cd5 ♗d8 13 ♕h5 gave White a typical light-squared bind in the game Blau-Plater, Hilversum 1947, while 9...0-0 10 ♗xf6 ♗xf6 11 ♕xd6 ♗e6 12 0-0-0 ♗g5+ 13 ♔b1 ♕f6 14 ♕c5 left Black with inadequate compensation for his pawn in Estrin-Goldenov, USSR 1956) 10 ♗xf6 ♗xf6 11 ♘d5 b5 12 ♘cb6 ♖b8 13 ♘xc8 ♖xc8 14 c3 ♘e6 15 a4! gave White a clear advantage in Averbakh-Korchnoi, USSR Championship 1950.

b) 8...d5 is well met by 9 ♘xd5 ♗xa3 10 bxa3 ♕a5+ 11 ♕d2 (11 ♗d2 is also possible) 11...♕xd2+ 12 ♔xd2 ♘xd5 13 exd5 ♘d4 14 ♗d3 with an extra pawn and the two bishops.

9 ♘c4 ♖c8 10 ♗xf6 gxf6

Black can avoid weakening his pawn structure with 10...♕xf6 but this loses time. White can keep an edge with 11 ♘b6! (and not 11 ♘xd6+ ♗xd6 12 ♕xd6 ♖d8 13 ♕c5 ♘d4 14 ♗d3 ♕g5 with excellent counterplay) 11...♖b8 12 ♘cd5 ♕d8 13 c3. Tolnai-Honos, Hungarian Team Championship 1995 continued 13...♗e7 14 g3 0-0 15 ♗g2 ♕e8 16 0-0 ♔h8 17 a4 ♗d8 18 b4 ♘e7 19 a5 ♕c6 20 ♖c1 with a clear edge.

11 ♘e3 ♗h6

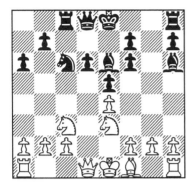

By exchanging off the knight on e3, Black rids himself of his bad bishop and weakens White's control of the d5- and f5-squares. Even so, it does not seem quite enough to equalise. An alternative is 11...♘e7, after which Anand-Morovic, Las Palmas 1993 continued 12 ♗d3 ♗h6 13 0-0 ♗xe3 14 fxe3 ♛b6 15 ♛c1 ♘g8! 16 ♔h1. Now Morovic suggested 16...h5!? (in the game he stood worse after 16...♛c5 17 ♛d2 h5 18 ♖ad1 h4 19 h3 ♔f8 20 ♛e2), after which 17 ♘d5 is well met by 17...♗xd5 18 exd5 ♘e7 19 e4 f5! with chances for both sides. In my view White should keep the tension with 17 ♖b1!? or 17 a3, when the defects in Black's position remain.

12 ♗d3 ♗xe3

Black can transpose into the note to Black's 11th with 12...♘e7.

13 fxe3 ♛b6 14 ♛c1 ♘a5?!

A natural move, going for counterplay on the c-file, but White's play on the f-file may prove more effective. Black can still transpose into the note to his 11th with 14...♘e7. Another way to defend the f6-pawn is with 14...h5 15 0-0 ♖h6, but this still seems better for White after 16 ♔h1 ♘e7 17 a3 h4 (Oll-

Sermek, Moscow Olympiad 1994) and now 18 h3! leaves Black struggling.

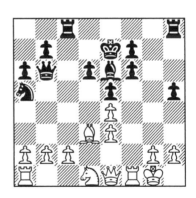

15 0-0 ♔e7 16 ♛e1 h5

16...♘c4 17 ♘d1 would transpose back into the game but this may represent a more accurate move order from Black's point of view as it avoids the potential perils of 16...h5 17 b3.

17 ♘d1

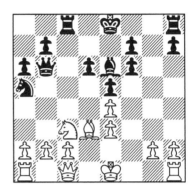

17 b3 was played in a game Ki.Georgiev-Shirov, Biel 1992 when Karpov suggested that Black had to play 17...♖xc3! (the game resulted in a quick defeat for Black after 17...♛c5 18 ♘d5+ ♗xd5 19 exd5 ♛xd5 20 ♖d1 ♛cg8 21 ♛f2 ♖h6 22 ♗g6!! 1-0) 18 ♛xc3 ♛xe3+ 19 ♔h1 ♘c6 20 ♖ae1 ♛c5 21 ♛d2 (21 ♛xc5 dxc5 leaves Black with good

compensation for the exchange because of the bad bishop on d3) 21...♞b8! 22 ♖f3 ♞d7, when it is very difficult for White to make progress.

17...♞c4?!

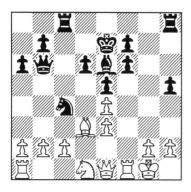

Going for active counterplay but the knight ends up the poor a3-square. Maybe 17...♕c7 is worth a thought, intending to bring the knight back via c6 to b8 and then out again to d7. That f6-pawn needs protecting.

18 b3 ♞a3 19 c4 ♕c5 20 ♞c3 b5 21 ♞d5+ ♝xd5 22 cxd5 ♕c3

After 22...♞c2 there follows 23 ♗xc2 ♕xc2 24 ♕h4 ♖h6 25 ♖xf6 etc.

23 ♕h4 ♖h6 24 ♖xf6 ♖xf6 25 ♖f1 ♖f8 26 ♕xf6+ ♚d7 27 ♖d1 ♕b2 28 h4!

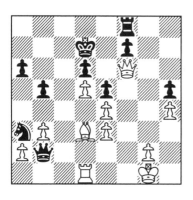

A very deep move, setting up an eventual endgame win based on the poor position of Black's knight.

28...a5 29 ♕f1 ♚e7 30 ♖c1 ♕d2 31 ♖c7+ ♚d8 32 ♖c1! ♕xc1+ 33 ♖xc1 ♚d7 34 ♖c6 ♖c8 35 ♖xc8 ♚xc8 36 g4 ♚d7 37 gxh5 ♚e7 38 ♚g2 1-0

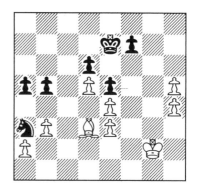

An elegant game by Prasad.

Game 37

Spassky-Gheorghiu

European Team Ch., Bath 1973

1 e4 c5 2 ♞f3 ♞c6 3 d4 cxd4 4 ♞xd4 ♞f6 5 ♞c3 e5 6 ♞db5 h6?!

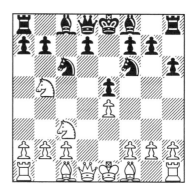

The most radical way of preventing the move ♗g5 and therefore maintaining an important guardian of the d5-

square. But White's reply gains the bishop pair, which is an important factor in the endgame.

Black has tried several other moves but all of them leave White in command:

a) 6...a6 7 ♘d6+ ♗xd6 8 ♕xd6 ♕e7 9 ♕d1!

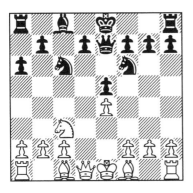

gains the bishop pair and leaves Black to worry about the possibility of ♗c1-g5.

b) 6...♗c5 is well met by 7 ♗e3! ♗xe3 8 ♘d6+ ♔f8 9 fxe3 ♕b6 10 ♘c4 ♕c5 11 ♕d6+ ♕xd6 12 ♘xd6

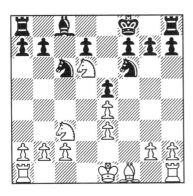

and White was clearly better in the game Bivsev-Abramov, USSR 1951.

c) 6...♗b4 7 a3 once again gains the two bishops.

7 ♘d6+ ♗xd6 8 ♕xd6 ♕e7

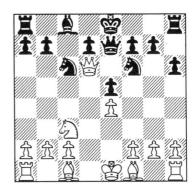

9 ♘b5!

Ex-world champion Spassky introduced this move in this game, which essentially puts the whole line out of business. Black gets a truly miserable endgame position in which the best he can hope for is a draw.

9...♕xd6 10 ♘xd6+ ♔e7 11 ♘f5+ ♔f8 12 b3! d5

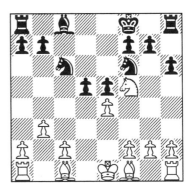

Perhaps Black should at least get some material for his trouble and play 12...♘xe4, though his position looks unenviable after 13 f3 (13 ♗a3+ ♔g8 14 ♘d6 ♘xd6 15 ♗xd6, as given by Maric, seems less effective to me) 13...♘f6 14 ♗a3+ ♔g8 15 ♘d6 with a strong bind and the threat of 16 ♗c4.

13 ♗a3+ ♚g8 14 exd5 ♘xd5 15
♘d6 ♖b8 16 ♗c4 ♗e6 17 0-0-0 ♘f4

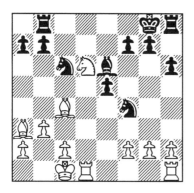

It's already difficult to give Black
good advice. White has the bishop pair,
a queenside majority and a lead in development, and it seems only a question
of time before Black loses material. Had
he played the alternative 17...♘c3, there
would follow the continuation 18 ♗xe6
fxe6 19 ♖de1 ♘xa2+ 20 ♚b2 ♘ab4 21
♗xb4 ♘xb4 22 ♖xe5 with a clear advantage.

18 g3 ♗xc4 19 ♘xc4 ♘e2+ 20 ♚b2
b5 21 ♖he1

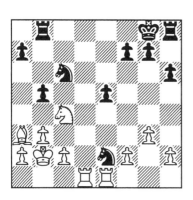

21...bxc4

After the alternative 21...♘xg3 there
is the powerful reply 22 ♗d6! ♖d8 23
♘xe5 ♘xe5 24 ♗xe5 ♖xd1 25 ♖xd1

♘e4 26 f3 ♘g5 27 f4 followed by 28
♖d7.

22 ♖xe2 f6 23 ♖e4 cxb3 24 cxb3!
♚h7 25 ♖c4 ♖hd8 26 ♖xd8 ♘xd8 27
♗c5 a6 28 ♚c3

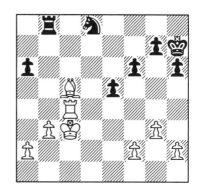

Instructive use of the king. Together
with his superior minor piece and
queenside pawn majority, this will prove
decisive.

28...♚g6 29 a4 ♚f7 30 ♗e3 ♚e6 31
♖c7 ♖b7 32 ♖c8 ♖d7 33 ♗b6 ♘b7
34 ♖a8

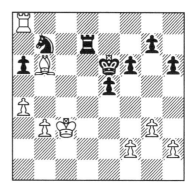

The white rook has successfully in-
filtrated the black queenside and the a-
pawn is now falling.

34...♖d6 35 a5 ♖c6+ 36 ♚b4 ♘d6
37 ♖xa6 ♘c8 38 ♚b5 ♚d5 39 ♖a8
♖c3 40 ♚b4 ♖c2 41 ♗e3 1-0

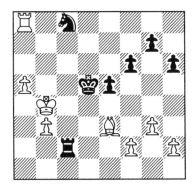

Summary

The Sveshnikov is a tough nut to crack, but White should get good practical results with the line featured here. It seems that Black has problems to solve after 13...♗e6!? (as in Game 35) and then 15...a5 because of the dangerous 17 ♕e2!. Perhaps Krasenkow or some other specialist has discovered a way for Black to get counterplay but it certainly is not easy. His position is still full of weaknesses even after he eliminates the horrible doubled f-pawns.

The recent attempts to rehabilitate 8...♗e6 seem to be floundering because of Game 36. Perhaps there will be some further research into 11...♘e7 but Black's position still looks uncomfortable here if White plays the game methodically.

Finally, it seems unlikely that 6...h6 will clamber its way out of the theoretical dustbin.

CHAPTER SEVEN

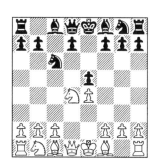

The Löwenthal, Kalashnikov and Other ...e5 Lines

With the upsurge in popularity of the Sveshnikov Variation, it was probably inevitable that some efforts would be made on behalf of the Löwenthal (1 e4 c5 2 ♘f3 ♘c6 3 d4 cxd4 4 ♘xd4 e5) and other ...e7-e5 lines.

There has indeed been a major development in that it was discovered that 5 ♘b5 d6!?

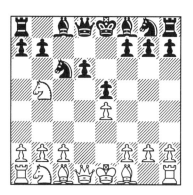

might be quite playable for Black, especially after the once-feared 6 c4. As a result it became all the rage and was dubbed the 'Kalashnikov Variation'. Whilst it was not playable against the Sveshnikov, a good method of combat-

ing the Kalashnikov is to play 6 g3 as in Nunn-van der Wiel (Game 38).

There have also been some developments in the old form of Löwenthal Variation in which Black meets 5 ♘b5 with 5...a6 6 ♘d6+ ♗xd6 7 ♕xd6 ♕f6,

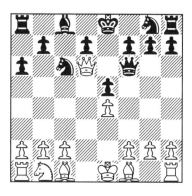

but some of these have been for White. The simple and economical route to an advantage is with 8 ♕xf6 ♘xf6 9 ♘c3, after which neither 9...♘b4 (Game 39) nor 9...d5 (Game 40) allows Black to obtain equality.

In Kiik-Wehmeier (Game 41) we see an unusual ...e7-e5 line which is probably much better than its reputation. As this opening does not have a name, I will take this opportunity to call it the 'M-16 Variation'. The theoretically approved 5 ♗b5+ does not impress me, but Kiik's 5 ♘e2 seems very logical. The game transposes into positions akin to the Najdorf and Classical Variations and a direct transposition is possible. Wehmeier gives the game independent significance with his 6...♗e6 but falls well short of equality.

> ### Game 38
> ### Nunn-Van der Wiel
> Wijk aan Zee 1991

1 e4 c5 2 ♘f3 ♘c6 3 d4 cxd4 4 ♘xd4 e5 5 ♘b5 d6 6 g3

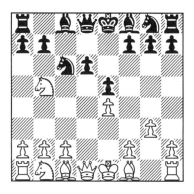

6...♗e7

The immediate 6...♘f6 allows 7 ♗g5. Black can try to escape the strategically undesirable consequences of his knight being exchanged with 7...♕a5+ but after 8 ♕d2 ♘xe4 9 ♕xa5 ♘xa5 White gets a powerful initiative with 10 ♗e3!.

Black has tried the exotic 6...h5. In Nunn-Short, Wijk aan Zee 1990 White ignored Black's demonstration with 7 ♘1c3 (there is also an argument for 7 h4 as the inclusion of these two h-pawn

moves may well favour White) and after 7...a6 8 ♘a3 h4 9 ♗g2 h3 10 ♗f1 b5 11 ♘d5 ♘ce7 12 ♗g5 f6 13 ♗e3 ♘xd5 14 ♕xd5 ♖b8 15 0-0-0 had a huge advantage.

The aggressive but loose-looking 6...f5 ran into all sorts of trouble in Hamdouchi-Tregubov, Cap d'Agde 2000. After 7 ♘1c3 a6 8 ♗g5! ♗e7 9 ♗xe7 ♔xe7 10 ♘c7! ♖b8 11 ♗c4! Black's king was in the middle and coming under fire.

7 ♗g2

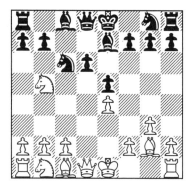

7...♘f6

7...a6 8 ♘5c3 ♘f6 transposes back into the game after 9 h3. An independent alternative is 7...♗e6 but this still looks better for White after 8 ♘1c3 (and not 8 0-0? ♗c4) 8...a6 (8...♘f6 9 ♘d5 0-0 10 0-0 ♕c8 11 a4 was also nice in Ivanchuk-Maidla, Tallinn 1996) 9 ♘a3 ♖c8 (9...♘f6 10 ♘d5 b5 11 c3 0-0 12 ♘c2 is also slightly better for White, as in Yemelin-Bogachkov, St. Petersburg 2001). Now in Nunn-Fauland, European Team Championship, Haifa 1989 Black met White's 10 0-0 with 10...♘b4 11 ♘d5 ♘xd5 12 exd5 ♗d7 and obtained a reasonable game, but 10 ♘d5 looks good for White.

8 h3

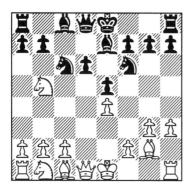

Following 8 0-0 Black would play 8...♗g4, after which 9 ♕d3 (or 9 f3 ♗e6) 9...a6 10 ♘5c3 ♘b4 is awkward.

8...a6 9 ♘5c3 b5 10 0-0

Certainly the most natural move, but it might be worth considering 10 ♘d2!?. Then 10...0-0 (or 10...♗e6 11 ♘d5) can be met by 11 ♘d5 as after 11...♘xd5 12 exd5 ♘a5 White has 13 b4! with a clear advantage.

10...0-0 11 ♗e3?!

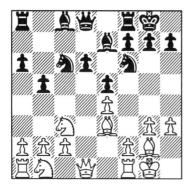

A 'natural' developing move, but it's not clear that the bishop is that well placed on this square. It is more logical to play 11 ♘d5 ♘xd5 12 exd5 ♘a5 13 b3, which is given as equal by van der Wiel. I prefer White because of Black's

badly placed knight on a5 which may struggle to find a decent career (after a later ...♘b7 White may, for example, play b3-b4).

11...♘a5!? 12 ♘d2 ♗b7 13 ♘d5 ♘xd5 14 exd5 ♖c8?!

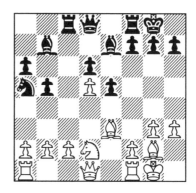

Preparing to meet 15 b4 with 15...♘c4 but the problems now come from another direction. Black should play 14...f5, after which 15 b4! f4 16 gxf4 exf4 17 ♗d4 ♘c4 18 ♘xc4 bxc4 produces a complex position in which both sides have chances.

15 a4! f5

In playing 14...♖c8 Black might have missed that 15...b4 is strongly answered by 16 ♕g4!. The result is that White gets the a-file.

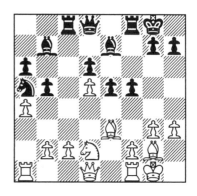

16 axb5 axb5 17 ♕e2! ♘c4

17...♖xc2 is bad because of 18 ♕xb5 f4 19 ♗b6, while if Black plays 17...f4 18 gxf4 exf4 19 ♗d4 ♖xc2 there is 20 ♖xa5! ♕xa5 21 ♕xe7 etc.

18 ♘xc4 bxc4 19 ♖a7 ♗a8 20 ♖fa1 e4!

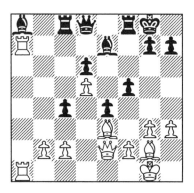

Black desperately needs some counterplay and the d5-pawn is the only weakness in White's position.

21 ♕d2 ♗f6 22 ♗d4 ♖f7 23 ♖xf7 ♔xf7 24 ♖a7+ ♔g8

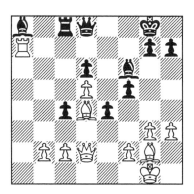

25 ♗f1

An interesting alternative is 25 g4!?, attempting to undermine the e4-pawn. According to Nunn Black should answer this with 25...♗xd4 26 ♕xd4 ♕f6 27 ♕xf6 gxf6 28 ♖a5 ♔g7!? 29 gxf5

♔h6 30 ♗xe4 ♔g5, when his active pieces should enable him to get a draw.

25...♗xd4 26 ♕xd4 ♕f6 27 ♕xf6 gxf6

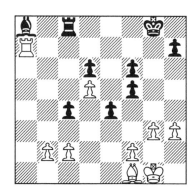

28 ♖d7!

A better try than 28 ♗xc4 ♖xc4 29 ♖xa8+ ♔g7 30 c3 ♖c5, which leads to a drawish rook endgame.

28...♗xd5 29 ♖xd6 ♗f7 30 ♖xf6 ♖b8

There is an attempt to pull off a swindle with 30...c3!? 31 b4 ♗b3 but this is refuted by 32 ♗a6! ♖c7 33 b5! ♗xc2 34 b6 etc.

31 ♖c6 ♖b4! 32 ♖c7

Black was trying to provoke his opponent into playing 32 c3?! as after 32...♖xb2 33 ♗xc4 ♗xc4 34 ♖xc4 ♔g7 White is unable to bring his king to e2. Had Black played 31...♖xb2, the c-pawn would have provided the necessary cover.

32...♗e6 33 h4 ♔f8 34 ♖xh7 ♖xb2 35 h5

Results often hinge on small details. In this position White should first play 35 c3! as after 35...♖c2 36 h5 ♖xc3 (36...e3! is the best try and may yet hold the draw) 37 h6 ♔g8 38 ♖e7 ♗d5 39 ♖e5 ♗f7 40 ♖xf5 ♗g6 41 ♖c5 Black cannot push his c-pawn as he does in the game.

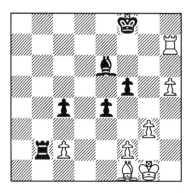

35...♖xc2 36 h6 ♔g8 37 ♖e7 ♗d5 38 ♖e5 ♗f7 39 ♖xf5 ♗g6 40 ♖c5 c3! 41 ♖c7?!

White should settle for a draw at this point with 41 ♗c4+ ♔h7 42 ♗b3 ♖c1+ 43 ♔g2 etc. By pushing for the win he could have lost.

41...♔h8 42 g4 ♖c1 43 ♔g2 c2 44 g5 ♗f5! 45 ♗e2 e3 46 ♗h5??

Given an exclamation mark by Van der Wiel, but White should play simply 46 ♖c5, after which 46...♖e1 47 ♖xf5 ♖xe2 48 ♖f8+ ♔h7 49 ♖f7+ ♔g6 50 ♖g7+ ♔f5 51 ♖f7+ ♔xg5 52 h7 is a draw.

46...exf2?

46...e2 would force White to find 47 ♗xe2 ♖e1 48 ♗g4!, with a draw still resulting after 48...♗e4+ 49 f3 ♗d3 50 ♖c8+ ♔h7 51 ♖c7+ ♔g8 52 ♖c8+ etc. However, Black could win with 46...♖b1! 47 fxe3 (or 47 g6 c1♕ 48 g7+ ♔h7 49 ♖xc1 ♖xc1 50 ♗f7 ♗e4+! 51 f3 ♗xf3+ 52 ♔g3 ♖g1+) 47...c1♕ 48 ♖xc1 ♖xc1 49 ♔g3 ♖c4 etc.

47 ♔xf2 ♖h1 48 ♗f7 c1♕ 49 ♖xc1 ♖xc1 50 g6 ♗xg6 51 ♗xg6 ♖c6 ½–½

Game 39
R.Byrne-Evans
US Championship, South Bend 1981

---

1 e4 c5 2 ♘f3 ♘c6 3 d4 cxd4 4 ♘xd4 e5 5 ♘b5 a6

This is Löwenthal's move, which gives up the bishop pair in return for quick development.

6 ♘d6+ ♗xd6 7 ♕xd6 ♕f6

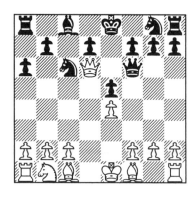

8 ♕xf6

The bishop pair can be especially effective in the endgame, so it makes a lot of sense to exchange queens. Besides being the simplest line, the resultant positions are not very pleasant for Black. White has tried a number of other moves including 8 ♕c7, 8 ♕a3, 8 ♕d2 and 8 ♕d1, but these tend to lead to tricky play in which a specialist in the Löwenthal is likely to be well prepared.

8...♘xf6 9 ♘c3

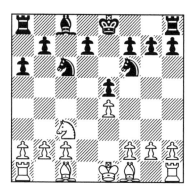

9...♘b4

Black must try for active counterplay before the two bishops make their presence felt. For 9...d5 see the next game.

10 ♗d3!

Once again the simple and economical move. 10 ♔d2 is also possible but this seems to leave White's king precariously placed after 10...d5 11 a3 d4 12 axb4 dxc3+ 13 ♔e3 ♘g4+ 14 ♔e2 f5 etc.

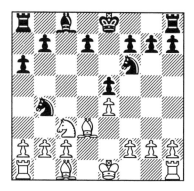

10...h6!?

This prevents ♗g5 but loses time and

leaves White slightly better. Alternatives include:

a) The sharpest try is 10...d5 11 exd5

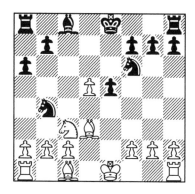

11...♘xd3+ (11...♘fxd5 12 ♘xd5 ♘xd5 13 ♗d2 ♗e6 14 0-0-0 f6 15 ♗a5 gave White a two-bishop edge in Nunn-TASC ♖30, The Hague 1994) 12 cxd3 ♗f5 13 ♗g5! ♗xd3 14 ♖d1 ♗b5? (14...♗f5 is better, but still good for White after 15 ♗xf6 gxf6 16 f3) 15 ♗xf6 gxf6 and now 16 ♘e4 won a pawn in De Firmian-Hreinsson, Gausdal 1999.

b) 10...0-0 11 ♗g5 ♘xd3+ 12 cxd3 d6 13 ♗xf6 gxf6 14 f4 b5 was played in Hübner-Pinkus, Germany 1997. Now 15 0-0 seems strong (in the game White played 15 ♘d5 ♔g7 16 ♖f1 ♗e6 17 ♘e3 but Black managed to draw with 17...exf4 18 ♖xf4 ♖ad8 followed by 19...d5).

c) 10...♘xd3+ 11 cxd3 d6 12 ♗g5 ♗e6 is an attempt to be solid, but White keeps the initiative with 13 f4! exf4 14 ♗xf6 gxf6 15 0-0 f5 16 exf5 ♗xf5 17 ♘d5 ♖c8?! (17...♔d8 is better, when White still has an edge because of his superior pawn structure) 18 ♖ae1+ ♔f8? (18...♗e6 is best, but still unpleasant after 19 ♘xf4 ♔e7 20 d4) 19 ♘e7 ♖c5

20 d4 and White won the exchange in Panchenko-Vladimirov, USSR 1975.

d) 10...b6 11 b3 d6 12 ♗a3 ♘xd3+ 13 cxd3 with a further split:

d1) After 13...♔d7 White can make life unpleasant for Black with 14 ♖d1 ♖e8 15 d4 ♘xe4 (15...exd4 16 ♖xd4 is also strong) 16 ♘xe4 exd4 17 ♖xd4 f5 18 0-0 ♖xe4 19 ♖xd6+ ♔c7 20 ♖c1+ ♔b7 21 h3.

d2) 13...♔e7 14 f4 ♔e6 (after 14...exf4 there is 15 e5!) 15 f5+ ♔e7 16 ♖d1 ♖e8 17 d4 exd4 18 ♖xd4 ♔f8 19 ♗xd6+ ♔g8 20 0-0 b5 21 e5 with a continuing initiative.

11 b3!

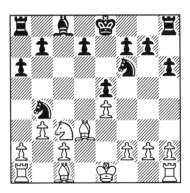

White is also slightly better after 11 ♗e3 ♘xd3+ (11...d6 12 0-0-0 ♗e6 13 ♗e2 was clearly better for White in Radulov-Forintos, Bulgaria 1981) 12 cxd3 d6 13 f3!? ♗e6 14 d4 because of his extra space, but Byrne's move is much stronger.

11...d6

11...d5 12 ♘xd5 ♘fxd5 13 exd5 ♘xd5 (13...♘xd3+ 14 cxd3 leaves White a pawn up) 14 ♗b2 gives White a typical two bishop endgame edge, but this would be better than what now happens.

12 ♗a3 ♘xd3+ 13 cxd3 ♔e7

After 13...♔d7 White turns the screw with 14 ♖d1 intending 15 d4, for example 14...♖e8 15 d4 ♘xe4 (15...exd4 16 ♖xd4 is also strong) 16 ♘xe4 exd4 17 ♖xd4 f5 18 ♖xd6+ ♔c7 19 0-0 ♖xe4 20 ♖c1+ ♔b8 21 ♖d8 ♔a7 22 f3 winning.

14 f4! ♔e6

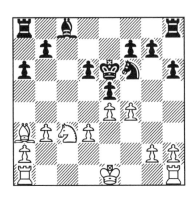

After 14...exf4 there is 15 e5.

15 f5+ ♔e7 16 ♖d1 ♖e8 17 d4 exd4 18 ♖xd4 ♔f8 19 ♗xd6+ ♔g8 20 0-0 b5 21 e5 1-0

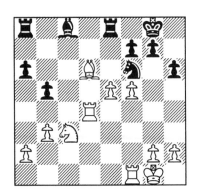

Game 40
Bykhovsky-Minic
Belgrade 1963

1 e4 c5 2 ♘f3 ♘c6 3 d4 cxd4 4

♘xd4 e5 5 ♘b5 a6 6 ♘d6+ ♗xd6 7
♕xd6 ♕f6 8 ♕xf6 ♘xf6 9 ♘c3 d5
10 ♗g5 ♘b4

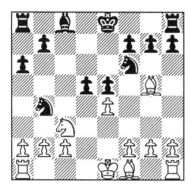

This move gives rise to some forcing play which ultimately leads to Black being a little worse in a rook endgame. He has instead tried a couple of alternatives:

a) 10...♘xe4 11 ♘xd5 ♘b4 12 ♗d3 (but not 12 ♘c7+ ♔d7! 13 ♘xa8 ♘xc2+) 12...♘xg5 (12...♘xd5 13 ♗xe4 is nice for White because of his bishop pair) 13 ♘c7+ ♔d7 14 ♘xa8 e4 15 a3 exd3 16 axb4 ♖e8+ 17 ♔d1 leaves Black with nothing for the exchange according to Gligoric and Sokolov.

b) 10...d4 11 ♗xf6 dxc3 12 ♗xg7 ♖g8 13 ♗h6! (13 ♗f6? cxb2 14 ♖b1 ♖g6 15 ♗h4 ♖g4! allowed Black to keep his extra pawn in Klein-Rosetto, Santa Fe 1960) 13...♘b4 14 0-0-0 ♘xa2+ 15 ♔b1 ♗e6 16 ♖d6 ♖g6 17 ♗e3 ♘b4 18 ♗c5, followed by capturing on c3, leaves White a good pawn up (Gligoric and Sokolov).

11 ♗xf6 gxf6 12 ♘xd5 ♘xc2+ 13 ♔d2 ♘xa1 14 ♘c7+ ♔e7 15 ♘xa8 ♗e6 16 ♘b6 ♗xa2

And not 16...♖d8+? as 17 ♗d3 wins a piece.

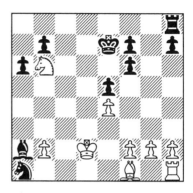

17 ♔c3 ♗e6 18 ♗c4 ♗xc4 19 ♘xc4 ♖c8 20 ♖xa1 b5 21 b3 bxc4 22 bxc4

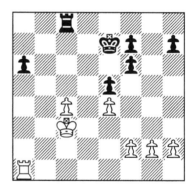

At first sight the position looks drawn, but White has the better rook, better king and superior pawn structure. In this game Black doesn't manage to hold the draw; whether he can do so with accurate play is a moot point.

22...♖c6 23 ♖a2

Protecting the second rank before probing with his king. Black's next move doesn't look right, as moving his h-pawn gives White the possibility of creating a passed pawn on the kingside.

23...h5? 24 ♔b4 ♖d6 25 ♔c5 ♔d7 26 h4 ♖c6+ 27 ♔b4 ♖d6 28 f3 ♔c7 29 ♔c3 ♔b6 30 ♖d2 ♖c6

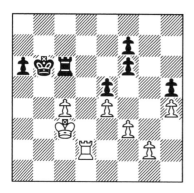

After the exchange of rooks White would get a passed h-pawn by playing g2-g4 which would enable him to win the game with his two separated passed pawns. But now White's rook gets to the 7th rank with decisive effect.

31 ♖d7 f5 32 exf5 ♖f6 33 g4 e4 34 fxe4 hxg4 35 h5 ♔c6 36 ♖d8 ♖h6 37 ♖g8 ♖xh5 38 ♔d4 ♖h4 39 ♖g7 g3 40 ♖xg3 ♖h8 41 ♖a3 ♖a8 42 ♔e5 ♔c5 43 ♔f6 ♔b4 44 ♖a1 ♖a7 45 ♖c1 ♔b3 46 e5 ♔b2 47 ♖e1 ♔c3 48 c5 ♔d4 49 e6 fxe6 50 fxe6 ♔xc5 51 e7 ♖xe7 52 ♖xe7 a5 53 ♔e5 a4 54 ♖a7 1-0

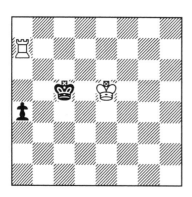

Black's a-pawn would need to be further advanced to let Black escape with a draw.

Game 41
Kiik-Wehmeier
Groningen 1991

1 e4 c5 2 ♘f3 d6 3 d4 cxd4 4 ♘xd4 e5!?

Although this has been widely condemned by theory, it seems quite playable to me.

5 ♘e2!

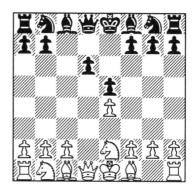

In keeping with the recipe of simplicity and economy, White leads the game down familiar paths by intending to fianchetto his king's bishop.

According to theory the strongest move is 5 ♗b5+ but I for one am totally unconvinced by this. For example, 5...♗d7 (or even 5...♘d7 6 ♘f5 a6 7 ♗xd7+ ♕xd7 8 ♘c3 ♕c6 9 ♘e3 ♗e6 10 ♕d3 ♘e7 11 0-0 g6 12 ♘ed5 ♗xd5 13 ♘xd5 ♘xd5 14 exd5 ♕c7 as in McShane-Wehmeier, Lippstadt 2000) 6 ♗xd7+ ♕xd7 7 ♘f5 (7 ♘f3 ♘f6 8 ♘c3 ♕c6 also looks very reasonable to me) 7...♘f6 8 ♘c3 ♘xe4! 9 ♘xg7+ ♗xg7 10 ♘xe4 d5 11 ♘g3 ♘c6 12 0-0 0-0-0 with an excellent game for Black in Masserey-Alexandria, Biel 1995.

5...♘f6 6 ♘bc3 ♗e6!?

Giving the game an independent flavour. 6...a6 7 g3 transposes into a Najdorf, while 6...♘c6 7 g3 leads to lines examined earlier, though in both cases White can also play 7 ♗g5!?.

7 g3 ♘c6

The logical follow-up to Black's last move is 7...d5, after which 8 exd5 ♘xd5 9 ♗g2 ♗b4 10 0-0 gives White a powerful initiative.

8 ♗g2 ♛d7 9 0-0 ♗e7 10 ♗g5 h6 11 ♗xf6 gxf6?

This ugly move intends to undermine the e4-pawn with ...f6-f5, but it looks slow compared with similar lines in the Sveshnikov Variation. Black should settle for the moderate inferiority that follows 11...♗xf6 12 ♘d5.

12 ♘d5 f5 13 exf5 ♗xf5 14 ♛d2 0-0-0

With kingside castling ruled out Black goes the other way. But the queenside will be no safe haven either.

15 b4 ♗g5 16 ♛c3 ♚b8 17 b5 ♘e7 18 b6 ♘xd5

There's no way to keep the b-file closed because 18...a6 is met by 19 ♛c7! ♚a8 20 ♘xe7 ♛xc7 (20...♗xe7 21 ♗xb7 mate) 21 bxc7 winning a rook

19 bxa7+ ♚a8 20 ♗xd5 ♖c8 21 ♛f3

♗xc2 22 ♖ab1!?

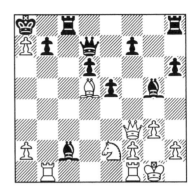

An interesting positional exchange sacrifice. White wants to be on that b-file and is willing to pay for the privilege.

22...♗xb1 23 ♖xb1 ♖c7 24 ♘c3 f5

After 24...♖xc3 25 ♛xc3 ♖c8 there follows 26 ♖xb7 ♛xb7 27 ♗xb7+ ♚xb7 28 ♛xc8+ ♚xc8 29 a8♛+ etc.

25 ♛d3 ♖h7?

Hereabouts Black starts playing very passively. At this point he should go for counterplay on the c-file with 25...♖hc8, after which 26 ♖b3 f4 27 ♗e4, intending 28 ♘d5, leaves White with compensation for the exchange. But it is far from being a foregone conclusion.

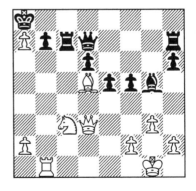

26 ♖b3 e4 27 ♛a6 ♗d8

White was threatening 28 ♘a4 which would, for example, follow 27...e3.

28 ♔g2 ♕c8?

Probably the losing move, possibly made in time-trouble. Black should go for counterplay with either 28...f4 or 28...e3, when things are still up in the air.

29 ♘b5! ♖c5 30 ♘xd6

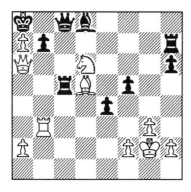

Suddenly everything converges on b7

and Black has no defence.

30...♕c6 31 ♗xc6 ♖xc6 32 ♕a3 ♗e7 33 ♖xb7 ♗xd6 34 ♕a4 ♖xb7 35 ♕xc6 ♗c7 36 ♕c5 ♗b6 37 ♕xf5 e3 38 fxe3 ♔xa7 39 ♔f3 ♖c7 40 e4 ♖c2 41 ♕h7+ 1-0

Summary

The critical point in our Kalashnikov treatment comes after the 11 ♘d5 improvement on Nunn-Van der Wiel. My own preference is for White because of Black's badly placed knight on a5.

The Löwenthal looks like a depressing prospect for Black after the exchange of queens, with Black fighting for a draw at best. The 'M-16 Variation' looks better than its reputation but we can return the game to familiar patterns by dropping the knight back to the e2-square.

CHAPTER EIGHT

The Dragon and other ...g6 Lines

The Sicilian Dragon was named thus because of its ferocious reputation and the apparent resemblance Black's formation has to the mythical beast. Although I don't quite see it myself, this opening has appealed to attacking players for decades. If White castles queenside you get the kind of sacrificial attacking play that Dragon specialists love, with the theory of many lines extending to 30 moves or more.

With the g3 lines you allow none of that and aim for the kind of slight advantage that drives most Dragoneers to distraction. One of the weaknesses of the Dragon formation is that Black does not cover the d5-square with any pawns and a Scheveningen style ...e7-e6 weakens the d6-pawn because the bishop is on g7 rather than e7. So after ♘d5 by White, Black usually has little choice but to capture with ...♘xd5. After that, an e-pawn recapture with exd5 gives White a space advantage and possible pressure on the e-file.

Against the most usual Dragon move order (1 e4 c5 2 ♘f3 d6 3 d4 cxd4 4 ♘xd4 ♘f6 5 ♘c3 g6) White plays 6 g3 and meets 6...♘c6 with 7 ♘de2!.

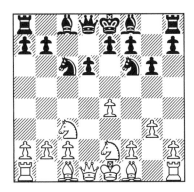

In my view White should avoid having the game simplified by exchanges because he has an advantage in space, and e2 is probably a better square for the knight than b3. Black then has to decide how he will try and obtain counterplay. Given time, White will play ♗g2, 0-0 and possibly ♖e1 and h2-h3 before planting his knight in the centre with ♘c3-d5.

In Yermolinsky-Smirin (Game 42) Black tries to interfere with White's development with 7...b6 8 ♗g2 ♗a6 but this does not cause White very much inconvenience. In Rechlis-Rachels (Game 43) Black also delays castling in order to try and cause White problems with 7...♗d7 8 h3 ♛c8 and now White must play 9 h3 to prevent ...♗h3.

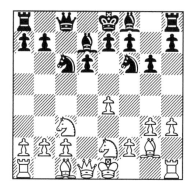

This does indeed delay White's castling, but meanwhile White has many other good moves. And as soon as Black takes the pressure off h3 by moving his queen from the passive c8-square, White will castle anyway.

In Rodriguez-Estevez Morales (Game 44) Black relies on simple development; his position is certainly sound enough but he has a distinct shortage of space. The attempt to gain counterplay with 9...♖b8 followed by a subsequent ...b7-b5 is a much more logical try, but Black should not get sidetracked into the passive 10...b6?! as in Ki.Georgiev-Shirov (Game 45). The most logical line is 10...a6, as in V.Georgiev-Berndt (Game 46), and to follow this up with 11...b5.

Generally speaking, the Accelerated Dragon (1 e4 c5 2 ♘f3 ♘c6 3 d4 cxd4 4 ♘xd4 g6) will transpose to these other variations after 5 ♘c3 ♗g7 6 ♘de2 followed by 7 g3. In Kaidanov-Salai (Game 47) I examine independent lines,

plus a good method of dealing with the Hyper-Accelerated Dragon (1 e4 c5 2 ♘f3 g6 3 d4 ♗g7!?).

Game 42
Yermolinsky-Smirin
Yerevan Olympiad 1996

1 e4 c5 2 ♘f3 d6 3 d4 cxd4 4 ♘xd4 ♘f6 5 ♘c3 g6 6 g3 ♘c6 7 ♘de2!

Keeping all the pieces on the board, which is generally good policy for the side with more space. White's subsequent plans are based around landing a knight on d5; if Black stops this with ...e7-e6 his d6-pawn will be weak.

7...b6

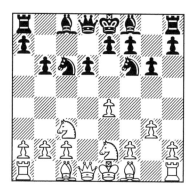

An interesting and unusual attempt to generate counterplay. For 7...♗d7 followed by ...♛c8 see Game 43.

8 ♗g2 ♗a6 9 0-0 ♗g7 10 h3

White's usual move, though it is by no means clear that it is necessary. In Kagan-Stisis, Israeli Championship 1990 White played 10 ♖e1 and kept an edge after 10...♖c8 11 ♘d5 0-0 12 ♗g5 ♘d7 13 ♖b1 h6 14 ♗e3 ♘de5 15 b3 e6 16 ♘df4 ♘b4 17 c4 ♗b7 (17...♘xa2?? 18 ♛d2) 18 ♛d2 etc.

10...0-0

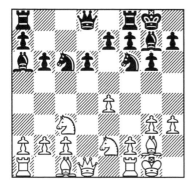

Black has also played 10...♖c8, after which 11 ♖e1 0-0 12 a4 ♘d7 13 ♘b5 ♗b7 14 ♖b1 a6 15 ♘a3 ♘c5 16 b3 ♘a7 17 ♘f4 b5 18 axb5 axb5 19 ♗d2 left White with a minimal advantage in Mokry-Miles, Reggio Emilia 1984. Yermolinsky has suggested 11 ♗g5 ♘d7 12 ♖e1 h6 13 ♗e3 ♘a5 14 ♗d4, when White has some central control.

11 ♗g5 h6

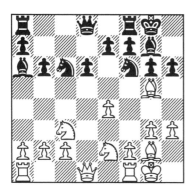

Another possibility is 11...♘d7 and, after 12 ♖e1, to weaken White's pawn structure with 12...♗xe2 13 ♕xe2 ♗xc3. Whilst this may indeed be playable, it is certainly not for the feint hearted. The absence of a dark-squared bishop leaves Black's kingside very weak.

12 ♗e3 ♘d7 13 ♖e1 ♖c8 14 ♕d2

Another idea is 14 ♖b1 to defend the b2-pawn.

14...♔h7 15 ♖ad1 ♘c5

In Bar-Stisis, Ramat Aviv 2000 Black attempted to improve on this with 15...♕c7, but after 16 ♘d5 ♕b8 17 b3 b5 18 ♘d4 ♘xd4 19 ♗xd4 e5 20 ♗e3 White was clearly better.

16 b3 ♗b7 17 g4!?

Commencing a general advance on the kingside. On his next move White intends to play 18 f4, so if Black wants some space in this sector this is his last chance to take some. After the immediate 17 f4 Black can apply restraint with 17...f5.

17...e5!? 18 f4!

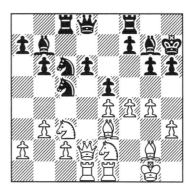

Rightly ignoring the pawn sacrifice. After 18 ♕xd6 Black gets powerful compensation with 18...♕h4 19 ♕d2 ♖fd8 20 ♕c1 ♘d4 etc., while after 18 ♘b5 there follows 18...♗a6 19 ♘xd6 ♖c7, intending ...♖d7.

18...exf4?!

An attempt to play dynamically, but White can force the queens off and emerge with a big advantage in the endgame. Before White has a chance to play 19 f5, Black should play 18...♘e6, although this too leaves White with the better game after 19 f5 ♘ed4 20 ♗xd4 ♘xd4 21 ♘xd4 exd4 22 ♘b5, intending to just capture on d4.

19 ♗xf4 ♖e8 20 ♕xd6

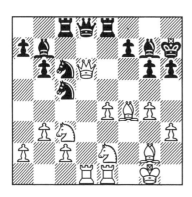

20...♕h4

After 20...♘b4 there follows 21 ♕xd8 ♖exd8 22 ♖xd8 ♖xd8 23 ♖c1, intending a2-a3 followed by ♘d5. If 20...♕xd6 21 ♗xd6 ♘b4 Black's counterplay grinds to a halt after 22 ♖c1 ♖cd8 23 ♗xc5 bxc5 24 a3 ♘c6 25 ♘d5 ♘d4 26 ♘xd4 ♗xd4+ 27 ♔f1 etc.

21 ♗g3 ♕g5 22 ♕d2 ♖cd8 23 ♕xg5 hxg5 24 ♖xd8 ♖xd8 25 ♘d5 ♖e8 26 c4!

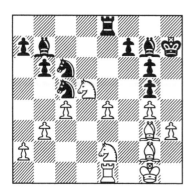

26...♘xe4?

Black hurries to restore material equality but this hastens his demise.

26...♖e6 looks like a more stubborn defence.

27 ♘ec3 ♘d6 28 ♖f1!

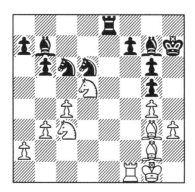

Even stronger than 28 ♖xe8 ♘xe8 29 ♘b5, which also leaves Black in a very difficult position.

28...♖d8

Black's position would also fall apart after 28...♘e5 29 ♘f6+ ♗xf6 30 ♖xf6 ♗xg2 31 ♔xg2, with multiple threats against the various weaknesses.

29 ♗xd6 ♖xd6 30 ♘e4 ♖d8 31 ♖xf7

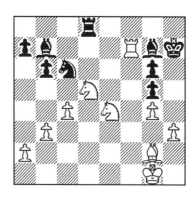

The harvest commences.

31...♗c8 32 ♖c7 ♘e5 33 ♘xg5+ ♔h6 34 ♘e4 g5 35 ♖xa7 b5 36 ♘xg5 bxc4 37 bxc4 ♖e8 38 ♖c7 ♗a6 39 ♖xg7 ♔xg7 40 ♘c7 ♖c8 41 ♘xa6 ♖xc4 42 ♘c5 ♖c2 43 a4 ♘c4

44 ♘ge6+ ♔f6 45 g5+ ♔e5 46 g6 1-0

1 e4 c5 2 ♘f3 d6 3 d4 cxd4 4 ♘xd4 ♘f6 5 ♘c3 g6 6 g3 ♘c6 7 ♘de2 ♗d7

Enacting this plan with 7...♗g4 8 ♗g2 ♕c8 is less good because 9 h3, which White will play anyway, gains a tempo on the bishop.

8 ♗g2 ♕c8 9 h3

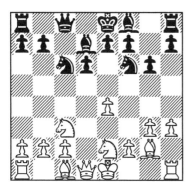

Preventing the exchange of light-squared bishops; after 9 0-0?! ♗h3 Black would be at least equal. Now White cannot easily castle as long as Black's queen is on c8, but he has plenty of other useful moves.

9...♗g7 10 a4!

Ruling out ...b7-b5 by Black. After 10 ♗e3 Black can consider 10...b5!?, after which 11 ♖c1 (11 ♘xb5 ♖b8 12 ♘xa7 ♘xa7 13 ♗xa7 ♖xb2 gives Black excellent counterplay) 11...b4 12 ♘d5 ♘xd5 13 exd5 ♘e5 14 b3 ♗b5 15 0-0 ♕a6 16 ♖e1 ♗xe2 17 ♕xe2 ♕xe2 18 ♖xe2 a5 brought about an equal endgame in

Marinkovic-Golubev, Belgrade 1991.

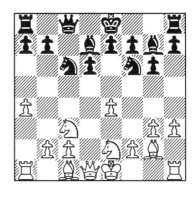

10...0-0

After 10...♘b4 there is 11 ♗e3, while 10...♘e5 gets nowhere after 11 b3.

11 ♗e3 ♖d8 12 ♕d2 ♘b4 13 ♖c1 ♗c6

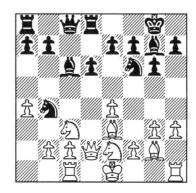

Playing for ...d6-d5. Black has also tried 13...a5, Short-Mestel, Hastings 1982/83 continuing 14 ♘d4 e6 15 b3 ♖a6 16 g4 ♗c6 17 0-0 e5 18 ♘xc6 ♖xc6 (18...bxc6 may be worth considering, though Black's knight on b4 may find it difficult to retreat) 19 ♘b5 ♖xc2 20 ♖xc2 ♕xc2 21 ♕xc2 ♘xc2 22 ♗b6, when White took the a-pawn and obtained a better endgame.

The wild-looking 13...h5?! led to the better game for White after 14 b3 e5?!

15 ♘b5 ♘c6 16 c4 in Short-Watson, Brighton 1982.

14 0-0 d5 15 e5 d4

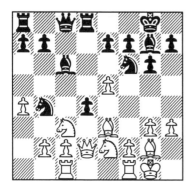

After 15...♘d7 16 f4 Black would have an awful version of the French, unless he were to sacrifice the d-pawn with 16...d4 for very little compensation.

16 ♗xd4 ♗xg2 17 ♔xg2 ♘c6 18 ♕e3

Simply 18 f4! would leave Black with inadequate compensation for the pawn. Now he gets some counterplay.

18...♘xd4 19 ♘xd4 ♘d5 20 ♘xd5 ♖xd5 21 ♘f3

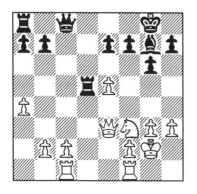

In this position 21 f4 can be met by 21...♕c4, which wins the a4-pawn. The text keeps White's extra pawn into the

endgame, though Black should now be able to hold a draw.

21...♕c5 22 ♕xc5 ♖xc5 23 c4 ♖ac8 24 b3 a6 25 ♖fe1 b5 26 axb5 axb5 27 ♖e4 e6 28 ♔f1 ♖a8 29 b4 ♖xc4 30 ♖exc4 bxc4 31 ♖xc4 ♖a1+ 32 ♔e2 ♖a2+?

32...♖b1 intending ...♗f8 would be a draw. Now White gets his b-pawn rolling by sacrificing f2.

33 ♔d3! ♖xf2 34 ♖c8+! ♗f8 35 ♘d2 ♖g2

After 35...♖f5 there follows 36 ♔e4 ♖f2 37 ♔e3 ♖f5 38 ♘f3 etc.

36 b5 ♖xg3+ 37 ♔c2 ♖a3 38 b6 ♖a2+ 39 ♔c1 ♖a1+ 40 ♘b1 1-0

Game 44
Am.Rodriguez-Estevez Morales
Sagua 1984

---

1 e4 c5 2 ♘f3 d6 3 d4 cxd4 4 ♘xd4 ♘f6 5 ♘c3 g6 6 g3 ♘c6 7 ♘de2 ♗g7 8 ♗g2 0-0 9 0-0 ♗d7

A natural move which focuses on development before committing to a specific plan.

Developing this bishop with 9...♗e6 is less good on account of 10 ♘f4 (10 ♘d5 may be somewhat premature because of 10...♗xd5 11 exd5 ♘e5 12 h3 ♕c7 with counterplay on the c-file) 10...♗c4 11 ♖e1, for example 11...e5 12 ♘fd5 ♘xd5 13 ♘xd5 f5 14 b3 ♗a6 15 ♗a3 f4 16 c3 ♕d7 17 ♘b4 ♘xb4 18 ♗xb4 ♖ad8 19 ♕d5+ ♔h8 20 c4 was strong for White in Svidler-Borge, Copenhagen 1991.

In the game Balashov-Dvoirys, Smolensk 1991 Black tried 9...♕a5 10 h3 ♕h5 but found himself under pressure after 11 ♘d5 ♘xd5 (and not 11...♗xh3?? 12 ♘df4) 12 exd5 ♘a5 13 ♘d4!? ♗xh3 14 ♕xh5 gxh5 15 ♗xh3 ♗xd4 16 ♖e1 – White has more than enough for the pawn.

For 9...♖b8 see Games 45-46.

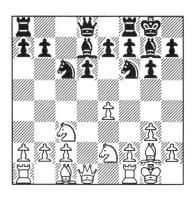

10 h3 ♖c8 11 a4

White will usually follow this with 12 ♘d5 but he waits for Black to commit his pieces whilst playing a move that he will probably need in any case. The alternatives are worth considering:

a) After 11 ♗e3 Gufeld and Stetsko recommend that Black goes for counterplay with 11...♘a5 (11...a6 12 ♘a4 b5 13 ♘b6 ♖b8 14 ♘xd7 ♘xd7 15 c3 gave White a useful pair of bishops in Kholmov-Chupin, St. Petersburg 1996) but this can be met by 12 a4 (12 b3 b5 is

indeed okay for Black) 12...♘c4 13 ♗c1 a6 14 b3 ♘a5 15 ♗d2 ♘c6 16 ♘a2!? e6 (16...b5 17 axb5 axb5 18 ♘b4 neatly blockades the b-pawn) 17 c4 b5 18 cxb5 axb5 19 ♗c3 bxa4 20 bxa4 d5 21 exd5 ♘xd5 22 ♗xg7 ♔xg7 23 ♘ac3

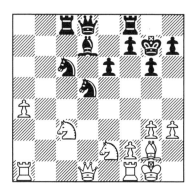

with White having an edge because of his passed a-pawn in Abramovic-Martinovic, Vrnjacka Banja 1983.

b) The immediate 11 ♘d5 can transpose back into 11 a4 lines after 11...♘xd5 12 exd5 ♘e5 13 a4 ♕c7 and now:

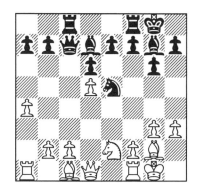

b1) 14 c3 b5 15 f4 ♘c4 16 axb5 ♗xb5 17 ♔h2 ♕b6 gave Black the initiative in Speelman-Peters, Hastings 1980/81.

b2) 14 ♘d4 ♕c5 15 c3 a6 16 ♖e1

≌fe8 and now 17 ≌a2 would keep a nice space advantage for White (the inferior 17 ♘c2 was played in Jansa-de Firmian, Vrnjacka Banja 1983).

11...♘b4

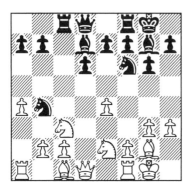

After 11...♘e5 12 ♘d5 (White may also consider another waiting move in 12 ≌a2) Black can transpose into variation 'b' of the previous note with 12...♘xd5 13 exd5 ♕c7 etc. Avoiding this exchange with 12...♘e8 was tried in Mestel-Silva, Malta 1980 but proved good for White after 13 ≌a2 e6 14 ♘e3 ♘c6 15 ♗d2 f5 16 exf5 gxf5 17 c4, and 12...≌e8 13 ≌a2 ♘xd5 14 exd5 left Black worse off than had he captured immediately in Andonov-Perenyi, Szolnok Mezogep 1985.

The superficially active 11...♕a5 ran out of steam after 12 ♘d5 ♘xd5 13 exd5 ♘e5 14 ♗d2 ♕c5 15 c3 ♕c4 16 b3 ♕a6 17 ♗g5 h6 18 ♗e3 ♘d3 19 ≌a2 in Reinderman-Ernst, Groningen 1996.

12 ♗e3 a5

At some point the knight will need this support or it will have to retreat with loss of time. In Marinkovic-Weidemann, Germany 1992 Black played 12...♕c7 13 ♕d2 ♘c6 (13...a5) and had a passive position after 14 ♘b5

♕b8 15 b3 b6 16 c4 ♘a5 17 ≌ab1 etc.

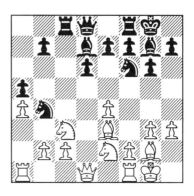

13 ♕d2 ♗c6

Less good is 13...♗e6 as after 14 ≌fd1 ♘d7 15 ♘d4 Black must constantly reckon with the possibility that White may saddle him with weak pawns by capturing on e6. Kudrin-Ivanovic, Titograd 1984 continued 15...♘e5 16 b3 ♘ec6 17 ♘db5 f5 18 ≌ac1 ♔h8 19 ♗h6 ♗xh6 20 ♕xh6 with the better game for White because of his well-coordinated pieces and Black's weakened structure.

14 ♘d4

Probably better than 14 ≌fd1, which gave Black active play after 14...♘d7 15 ♘d4 ♘b6 16 b3 d5 in Nunn-Mortensen, Helsinki 1986.

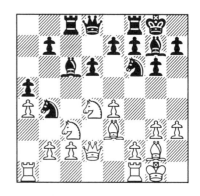

14...♕c7

Rodriguez mentioned the possibility of 14...d5 15 e5 ♘e4 but White seems to keep an edge with 16 ♘xe4 dxe4 17 c3 ♘d5 18 ♗xe4 ♗xe5 19 ♗h6 ♗g7 20 ♖fe1 and may well do even better with more ambitious ideas.

15 ♖ac1

Carefully protecting the c-pawn in anticipation of Black playing ...d6-d5. After 15 ♖fe1 d5 16 ♘db5 ♗xb5 17 ♘xb5 Black has 17...♕xc2.

15...♕b8

This time 15...d5 is well met by 16 ♘db5, after which 16...♕d7 17 ♖fd1 dxe4 18 ♕e2 ♕f5 (or 18...♕e8 19 ♗d4) 19 ♘d4 gives White the initiative.

16 f4 ♖fd8

Once White has played f2-f4, the sequence 16...d5?! 17 e5 is good for White as he has a large space advantage and does not have to worry about counterplay against a weak e-pawn.

17 ♕f2 ♗e8?!

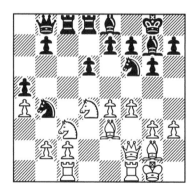

Black needs to secure his b-pawn with 17...♘d7 so as to meet 18 ♘b3 with 18...b6. After White's reply he must make a dubious exchange sacrifice or simply lose a pawn.

18 ♘b3! ♖xc3

After 18...♘d7 19 ♘xa5 ♘c5 20 ♗d4

White is simply a pawn up.

19 bxc3 ♘a2 20 ♖ce1 ♘xc3 21 ♗a7 ♕a8 22 ♘xa5

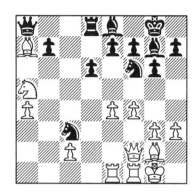

22...d5

And not 22...♘xa4?, when White wins on the spot with 23 e5!.

23 exd5 ♘fxd5 24 ♘b3 ♗xa4 25 ♗d4! ♗xb3

After 25...♗b5 White has 26 ♖a1 followed by 27 ♖fe1.

26 cxb3 e6 27 ♗xg7 ♔xg7 28 ♖c1?

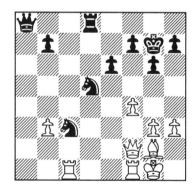

With this and his next move White starts to drift; he needs his pieces over on the kingside. The move 28 g4!, followed by 29 f5, would give White a winning attack.

28...♕a5 29 ♕b2? ♕a2! 30 ♖f2 ♕xb2 31 ♖xb2 b5! 32 ♗xd5

Black's pieces are coming to great squares and it will be very difficult for White to win the endgame. 32 b4 is met by 32...♖c8.

32...♘xd5 33 b4 h5! 34 h4 ♘b6 35 ♖c7

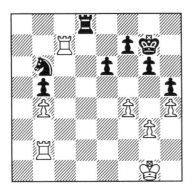

35...♘d5

The immediate 35...♖d3!? was also worth considering.

36 ♖b7 ♘c3 37 ♔g2 ♖d3 38 ♔h3 ♖d5 39 ♖b3 ♘e4 40 ♖e3 ♘f2+?

Giving White renewed winning chances. Simply 40...♘d6 would create an impenetrable blockade.

41 ♔g2 ♘g4

42 ♖c3!

And not 42 ♖xe6 because of 42...♖d2+ 43 ♔f1 (if 43 ♔f3? ♖f2+ 44

♔e4 ♖e2+; or if 43 ♔g1 then 43...♖d1+ 44 ♔g2 ♖d2+ draws) 43...♘h2+ 44 ♔e1 ♘f3+ with a draw by perpetual check.

42...♘h6 43 ♖cc7! ♖d2+ 44 ♔f1 ♖d3 45 ♔g2 ♖d2+ 46 ♔f1 ♖d3 47 ♔f2 ♖d2+ 48 ♔f3 ♖b2

After 48...♖d3+ there follows 49 ♔f2 ♖d2+ 50 ♔e3, escaping the checks.

49 ♖xb5 ♖b3+ 50 ♔g2 ♖b2+ 51 ♔f1 ♖b3 52 ♔g2 ♖b2+ 53 ♔g1 ♖b3 54 ♔f2 ♘f5 55 ♖d7!

The immediate 55 ♖bb7 can be met by 55...♘d6 56 ♖b6 ♘e4+ etc.

55...♖b2+

Or 55...♖xg3 56 ♖bb7 etc.

56 ♔e1 ♖b1+ 57 ♔d2 1-0

Game 45
Ki.Georgiev-Shirov
Pardubice 1994

---

1 e4 c5 2 ♘f3 d6 3 d4 cxd4 4 ♘xd4 ♘f6 5 ♘c3 ♘c6 6 g3 g6 7 ♘de2 ♗g7 8 ♗g2 0-0 9 0-0 ♖b8 10 a4 b6?!

In conjunction with 9...♖b8 this does not seem very logical, but it has nevertheless been played by a number of strong players. For the move 10...a6 see Game 46.

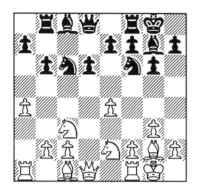

11 ♖e1

A solid and useful move. The line 11 h3 ♗b7 12 ♗e3 commits the queen's bishop quite early. Black can play 12...♘e5 and now:

a) 13 ♖a2 a6 14 ♘d5 b5 15 axb5 axb5 16 ♗b6 ♕d7 was okay for Black in V.Georgiev-Yrjola, Cappelle la Grande 1992.

b) 13 ♖e1 a6 14 ♖a2 e6 15 b3 ♕c7 16 ♕d2 ♖fd8 17 ♗g5 ♘ed7 with a solid position for Black in Mestel-Yrjola, Reykjavik 1990.

11...♗b7 12 h3

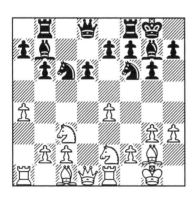

12...♘b4

After this White gains a structural advantage with the typical ♘d5 manoeuvre. In his notes Georgiev sug-

gested that 12...a6 13 ♗e3 ♘a7 might be better but then 14 a5 ♘c8 15 axb6 ♘xb6 16 b3 looks strong.

13 ♘d5 ♘bxd5 14 exd5 ♕c7 15 ♖a3!

Sending the rook to the e-file, from where it puts pressure on the backward e7-pawn.

15...♖fe8 16 ♖e3 ♖bc8 17 ♘c3 a6 18 ♖3e2

Another good line is 18 ♕e2 ♔f8 19 ♔h2, once again with strong pressure.

18...♔f8 19 ♗e3

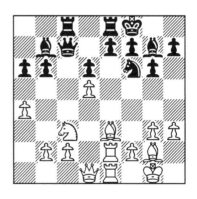

19...♕c4

After 19...♘d7 20 ♗d4 ♘e5 there would follow 21 f4 ♘c4 22 ♗xg7+ ♔xg7 23 ♕d4+ ♔g8 24 ♘e4 threatening 25 ♘f6+.

20 ♗xb6 ♘d7

Going for the b-pawn with 20...♕b4 21 ♗d4 ♕xb2 would leave Black defenceless after 22 ♕d3 followed by 23 ♖b1.

21 ♗e3 ♘c5 22 ♗g5 ♗e5 23 f4!

Sounding the charge. Another interesting possibility is 23 ♖xe5!? dxe5 24 d6 but this is less convincing after 24...exd6 25 ♕xd6+ ♔g8.

23...♗xc3 24 bxc3 ♖c7 25 f5!

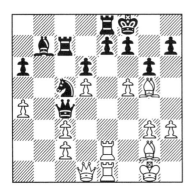

25...♕xc3

After 25...gxf5 26 ♕d2 White has too many threats.

26 ♖e3 ♕b2

And not 26...♕c4? because of 27 ♗h6+ ♔g8 28 ♕a1 f6 29 ♕xf6! exf6 30 ♖xe8+ ♔f7 31 ♖f8 mate.

27 f6 ♔g8 28 ♖xe7 ♖cxe7 29 ♖xe7 ♖f8 30 ♕e2

Another good way is 30 ♕d2, after which Black would be forced to give up the exchange with 30...h6 31 ♗xh6 ♕xf6 32 ♗xf8 ♔xf8. The game is rather similar.

30...♗xd5 31 ♗xd5 ♕d4+ 32 ♔h2 ♕xd5 33 ♗h6 ♘e6 34 ♗xf8 ♔xf8 35 ♕e3 ♕c6 36 ♕h6+?

Simpler would have been 36 ♕b3!, after which 36...♔g8 37 ♖xe6 fxe6 38

♕xe6+ ♔h8 39 c4 cuts out any counterplay and decides matters. Now White has to play very accurately.

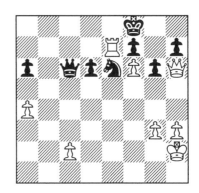

36...♔g8 37 ♕d2

And not 37 ♖xe6? because of 37...♕xc2+ 38 ♔g1 ♕b1+ 39 ♔f2 ♕f5+!, when White's king cannot escape the checks.

37...h6 38 h4

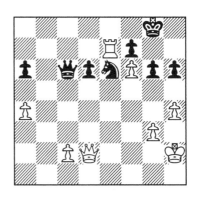

38...♕f3

Perhaps the immediate 38...g5!? was a better try. Now Black gets gradually ground down.

39 ♖d7 g5 40 ♖xd6 gxh4 41 ♕g2! ♕xf6 42 gxh4+ ♔f8 43 ♕g3 ♕f1 44 ♖d2 ♕c4 45 a5 ♔e7 46 ♖f2 ♕c5 47 ♕f3 ♕e5+ 48 ♔h1 f6 49 ♖e2 ♕xa5 50 ♕e4 ♕b6 51 c4 a5 52 ♕h7+

♔d8 53 ♕g8+ ♚e7

54 ♕g7+ ♚d6 55 ♖d2+ ♚e5 56
♖d5+ ♚f4 57 ♕xf6+ ♚g3 58 ♕g6+
♚h3 59 ♕f5+ 1-0

Game 46
V.Georgiev-Berndt
Bundesliga 2000

---

1 e4 c5 2 ♘f3 d6 3 d4 cxd4 4 ♘xd4
♘f6 5 ♘c3 g6 6 g3 ♘c6 7 ♘de2
♗g7 8 ♗g2 0-0 9 0-0 ♖b8

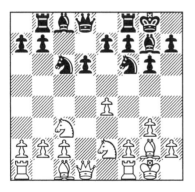

10 a4

The immediate 10 ♘d5?! is less good
as White does not get the open a-file.
After 10...b5 11 c3 b4! 12 cxb4 ♘xb4 13
♘xf6+ ♗xf6 14 ♗e3 ♕d7 15 ♕d2 ♗a6
Black had excellent counterplay in

Hnydiuk-V.Popov, Cappelle la Grande
2000.

10...a6 11 ♘d5

The immediate 11 h3 is also playable
but certainly less incisive.

11...♘d7

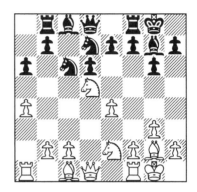

Arguably conceding ground a little
too early. The dynamic option is the
immediate 11...b5!? 12 axb5 axb5 and
now:

a) 13 h3 is adequately met by
13...♘d7 14 c3 e6 15 ♘e3 ♘c5 16 ♘d4
♗d7 17 ♘ec2 ♘xd4 18 ♘xd4 b4 as in
Rodriguez-Sutovsky, Argentina 1997.

b) 13 ♗e3 b4 14 ♘d4 ♘xd4 15 ♗xd4
♘xd5 16 exd5 ♗xd4 17 ♕xd4 ♗f5 18
♖a7 ♗xc2 19 ♖e1 ♖e8 20 ♗h3 b3 gave
White enough compensation for the
pawn but nothing more than that in
V.Atlas-Tischbierek, Dornbirn 2002.

c) 13 c3 b4! 14 ♘d4 ♘xd4 15 ♘xf6+
exf6 16 cxd4 f5 equalised for Black in
Kopylov-Nesis, correspondence 1997

d) White's most direct treatment is 13
♗g5, with a further split:

d1) 13...♘xd5 14 exd5 ♘e5 15 ♖a7
♖e8 was played in Grunina-Sukhareva,
St. Petersburg 2000, and now 16 h3
seems good, to prevent the exchange of
Black's light-squared bishop with

16...♗g4 and 17...♗xe2.

d2) 13...♘g4 14 c3 h6 15 ♗d2 ♘ge5 16 ♘d4 ♘xd4 17 cxd4 ♘c6 18 ♗e3 e5 19 dxe5 dxe5 20 ♕d2 gave White an edge in Marinkovic-Djoric, Yugoslav Team Championship 1996.

d3) Black can also avoid the exchange with 13...♘d7! 14 ♕c1 ♖e8! (Preparing to keep the dark-squared bishop. After 14...♘c5 White can simply exchange dark-squared bishops with 15 ♗h6, but he can also play 15 b4!? ♘e6 16 ♗h6 ♗xa1 17 ♕xa1 ♖e8 18 f4, followed by 19 f5, when White gets a strong attack for the sacrificed exchange.) 15 ♖d1 (15 ♗h6 ♗h8 16 ♖a2!? is worth considering) 15...♘c5 16 ♗h6 ♗h8.

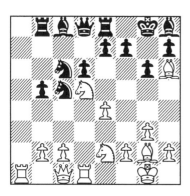

Now 17 b4?! ♗xa1 18 ♕xa1 ♘e6 was played in Al.Ivanov-Ernst, Gausdal 1991 but it is a dubious form of the exchange sacrifice because his rook on d1 does not support the advance of the f-pawn. Instead, 17 ♗e3 is the solid move that keeps a slight initiative.

12 c3 b5 13 axb5 axb5 14 ♗g5

Another possibility is 14 ♘d4 ♘xd4 15 cxd4 ♗b7 16 ♘b4 ♖a8 17 ♗e3 ♖xa1 18 ♕xa1 ♕b6 19 ♕d1, which maintained White's space advantage in Yanev-Ilchov, Bulgarian Team Cham-

pionship 1992.

14...♖e8

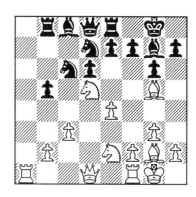

After 14...h6 15 ♗e3 e6 White keeps some pressure with the creative 16 ♘b4!?, when 16...♘xb4 17 cxb4 ♘e5 18 b3 produces a position in which the d6-pawn is much more of a liability than White's doubled b-pawns. Marinkovic-Paschall, Belgrade 2001 continued 18...♗b7 19 ♕d2 ♘g4 20 ♗d4 ♘f6 21 ♘c3 ♖a8 22 ♕d3 ♕b8 23 ♕xb5 e5 24 ♗e3 and White eventually won, while 18...♘g4 19 ♗d4 e5 20 ♗a7 ♖b7 21 ♘c3 was also good for White in V.Georgiev-Alonso, Madrid 2001.

15 ♘d4 ♘xd4 16 cxd4 ♗b7 17 ♘b4 ♖a8 18 ♕d2 ♖a4 19 b3 ♖xa1 20 ♖xa1 ♘c5?

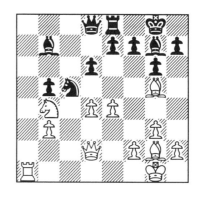

Black's position is certainly uncomfortable but this attempt to shoot his way out of trouble meets with a powerful reply. 20...♕b6 would have been preferable.

21 dxc5!! ♗xa1

Unfortunately for Black there's no way out. After 21...dxc5 there follows 22 ♘d5 ♗xd5 (22...♗xa1 23 ♘xe7+ wins the queen) 23 ♖d1 winning a piece.

22 c6 ♗a8 23 ♗h3 ♗f6

Or if 23...♕c7 there follows 24 ♗d7! with widespread carnage on the menu.

24 ♗d7 ♗xg5 25 ♕xg5 ♖f8 26 ♘d5 f6 27 ♕h6

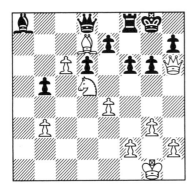

27...♗xc6

White was threatening 28 ♗e6+ followed by 29 c7 and after 27...♔h8 there follows 28 c7 ♕xd7 29 ♕xf8 mate.

28 ♗xc6 e6 29 ♘f4 1-0

After 29 ♘f4 ♕e7 there is 30 ♘xe6!.

Game 47
Kaidanov-Salai
Yerevan Olympiad 1996

1 e4 c5 2 ♘f3 ♘c6

Black can also consider the Hyper-Accelerated Dragon with 2...g6 3 d4 ♗g7 (3...cxd4 4 ♘xd4 ♗g7 5 ♘c3 ♘c6

6 ♘de2 leads back into normal lines), after which 4 dxc5 ♕a5+ 5 ♘fd2 ♕xc5 6 ♘b3 ♕c7 7 g3 d6 8 ♗g2 ♘c6 9 0-0 ♘f6 10 h3 0-0 11 ♘c3 brings about a familiar structure in which Black's queen is not well placed on c7.

3 ♘c3 g6 4 d4 cxd4 5 ♘xd4 ♗g7 6 ♘de2

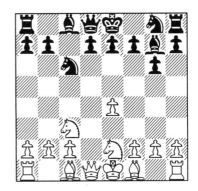

6...d6

Black has also tried to take advantage of the delayed ...d7-d6 to play ...d7-d5 in one go. But this opening of the centre appears to make the g2-bishop very strong: 6...♘f6 7 g3 d5!? 8 exd5 ♘b4 9 ♗g2 ♗f5 10 ♘d4 ♗g4 11 ♕d2 ♘bxd5 12 ♘xd5 ♘xd5 13 h3 ♗c8 14 ♘b3 led to much the better endgame for White in Fuchs-Litvinov, USSR 1968.

7 g3 ♗g4

7...♘f6 transposes into the Dragon lines already studied. The text is an independent line in which Black does not hurry to bring his knight to f6.

8 ♗g2 ♘d4

Black can also play 8...♘e5!? 9 0-0 (9 f4 leaves White's king misplaced after 9...♘f3+ 10 ♔f2 ♘d4) 9...♗f3 10 ♗xf3 ♘xf3+ 11 ♔g2 ♘e5 and now 12 ♘d5 e6 13 ♘dc3 ♘f6 was ineffective in the game Westerveld-Hendriks, Netherlands 1987, but 12 ♗f4!? ♘f6 13 ♗xe5! dxe5 14 ♕xd8+ ♖xd8 15 ♖fd1 0-0 16 a4 would give White the better endgame because of his queenside pawn majority.

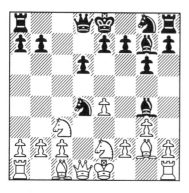

9 ♕d3 ♘xe2 10 ♘xe2 ♘f6

It seems difficult for Black to prevent White from achieving a promising Maroczy Bind set-up.

a) 10...♖c8 11 0-0 ♘f6 12 ♘f4 0-0 was played in Petkovic-Z.Nikolic, Becici 1993 and now 13 h3 ♗d7 14 c4 looks promising.

b) In Faibisovich-Michalek, Brno 1991 White was doing well after 10...♕c8 11 ♘f4 ♘f6 12 0-0 0-0 13 ♗e3 ♖e8 14 c4 ♘d7 15 f3 ♘e5 16 ♕e2 ♗d7 17 ♖ac1 etc.

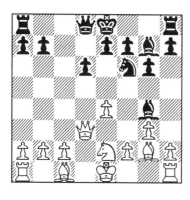

11 h3 ♗d7

The alternative is to give up the bishop pair with 11...♗xe2, but then 12 ♕xe2 ♘d7 13 0-0 ♕c7 14 c3 0-0 15 ♗g5 ♘c5 16 ♖ad1 a5 17 h4 gave White a pull in Dueball-Grünberg, Bundesliga 1987.

12 c4

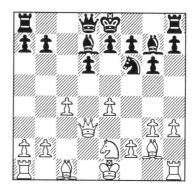

Setting up a 'Maroczy Bind' structure is the most promising way to play it for White. 12 0-0 0-0 13 a4 ♕c8 14 ♔h2 ♗e6 gave Black equality in Brenke-Archipov, Lippstadt 1993.

12...0-0 13 ♘c3 ♖c8

Kaidanov suggested that the immediate 13...a6!? may be better, but I prefer White in these positions even if Black arranges ...b7-b5 without losing a pawn.

14 ♗d2 ♕c7 15 b3 b5?!

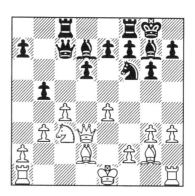

An unsound attempt to free his game to avoid suffering in a passive position. Black maintains material equality but unleashes White's bishops and gives him a dangerous queenside pawn majority.

16 ♘xb5 ♗xb5 17 cxb5 ♘xe4 18 ♖c1 ♘c5

Sacrificing the queen with 18...♕xc1+ leaves Black with inadequate compensation after 19 ♗xc1 ♖xc1+ 20 ♔e2.

19 ♕e2 ♕d7 20 ♗e3 ♕e6 21 ♖c4 ♖c7 22 ♖c2 ♖fc8 23 0-0

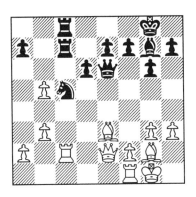

23...d5

If Black does nothing White will simply play 24 ♖fc1 and menace b3-b4.

24 ♖d1 ♘e4 25 ♖xc7 ♖xc7 26 ♗f4 ♖c8 27 ♗xe4 dxe4 28 ♕e3 ♖a8 1-0

Summary

Playing g2-g3 against the Dragon gives White good chances of obtaining a nagging space advantage, whilst sidestepping the tons of theory in which Dragoneers thrive. Georgiev-Berndt is the most important game to study, particularly the positions arising after 11...b5!?.

Black's attempts to mix things up early seem quite ineffective but White needs to know what he is doing. Games 42-43 are good models, as is Game 47 with regards to neutralising the Accelerated Dragon.

CHAPTER NINE

Other Lines

The variations in this chapter are not popular enough to merit separate coverage but they tend to crop up with greater frequency in club chess than they do at grandmaster level. The reason is that there is little theory on these lines, which makes them attractive to amateurs with little time for study.

First up is the ancient Four Knights Variation (1 e4 c5 2 ♘f3 ♘c6 3 d4 cxd4 4 ♘xd4 ♘f6 5 ♘c3 e6), which is sometimes used to transpose into a Pelikan after 6 ♘db5 d6 7 ♗f4 e5 8 ♗g5 a6 9 ♘a3 etc. The move with independent significance is 6...♗b4,

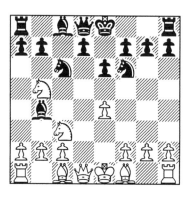

which is covered in Geller-Winants (Game 48). After obtaining the two bishops White tends to maintain a slight initiative but needs to play accurately. The position can easily become drawish should he play routine or automatic moves. White is unable to use a g3 setup in this line.

Gufeld's 4...♕b6 is quite a reasonable way to play a Scheveningen-style Sicilian without getting embroiled in lots of sharp theory.

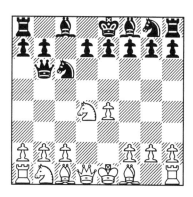

In Ivanov-Gufeld (Game 49) White sticks to his guns with 7 g3 and would probably have done better with 10 exd5.

The actual game was immensely complicated and White could easily have lost after accepting the rook sacrifice.

The Nimzowitsch Variation (1 e4 c5 2 ♘f3 ♘f6) features in Velickovic-Mnatsakian (Game 50), in which White plays the rare but promising 3 e5 ♘d5 4 g3!?. This resembles Rozentalis' treatment of the 2 c3 Sicilian in which he has met 1 e4 c5 2 c3 ♘f6 3 e5 ♘d5 with 4 g3!?, but obviously it is much better for White to have his knight on f3 rather than his pawn on c3.

Throughout the book I have recommended that White meets 1 e4 c5 2 ♘f3 e6 with 3 ♘c3 in order to avoid the unnecessary complications of the Pin Variation (3 d4 cxd4 4 ♘xd4 ♘f6 5 ♘c3 ♗b4). For the most part this means nothing more than a harmless transposition of moves, but in Lalic-Davies (Game 51) I attempted to give the game independent significance with (3 ♘c3) a6 4 g3 b5 5 d4!? b4.

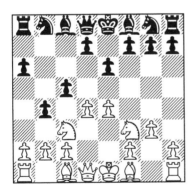

After this experience I would certainly be reluctant to repeat my play, but it is something you need to know about from White's point of view.

Finally there is the O'Kelly Variation (1 e4 c5 2 ♘f3 a6), which is much better than its reputation and has recently been tried by Grandmasters Csom and Onischuk (I have also been using it in offhand games). The supposed refutations, such as 3 c3 and 3 c4, do not impress me in the least. White should play 3 ♘c3, when 3...e6 4 d4 will lead to a Kan Variation. Black's attempt to attack e4 with 3...b5 4 d4 cxd4 5 ♘xd4 ♗b7 was severely punished in Shamkovich-Marchand (Game 52).

Game 48
Geller-Winants
Amsterdam 1987

---

1 e4 c5 2 ♘f3 ♘c6 3 d4 cxd4 4 ♘xd4 e6

The 'official' move order of the Sicilian Four Knights is 4...♘f6 5 ♘c3 e6, which leads back into the game.

5 ♘c3 ♘f6 6 ♘db5 ♗b4

Black often transposes into a Pelikan at this stage with 6...d6 7 ♗f4 e5 (7...♘e5 leaves Black in desperate trouble after 8 ♕d4) 8 ♗g5 a6 etc. The text is the old move that gives White the two bishops.

7 a3 ♗xc3+ 8 ♘xc3 d5 9 exd5 exd5

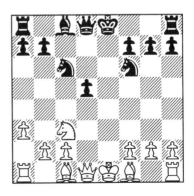

Accepting an isolated pawn, though with only one knight this is difficult for White to restrain, blockade and destroy. Instead he should attempt to use his bishop pair.

Alternatively Black can play 9...♘xd5 10 ♗d2! (10 ♘xd5 exd5 would leave Black very solidly placed, as he does not even need to worry about a pin on his f6 knight) and now:

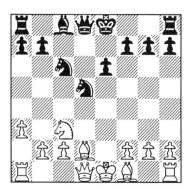

a) 10...e5 11 ♕h5 0-0 12 ♗d3 ♘f6 13 ♕h4 e4 14 ♗c4 ♘d4 15 0-0-0 ♗g4 16 ♗g5 ♗xd1 17 ♖xd1 ♖c8 18 ♗xf6 gxf6 19 b3, intending 20 ♘d5, gave White a winning attack in Tal-Peterson, Riga 1965.

b) 10...♕h4 11 ♕f3 0-0 12 0-0-0 ♘xc3 13 ♗xc3 e5 14 ♗d3 ♗g4 15 ♕e4 ♕h6+ 16 ♗d2 ♕g6 17 f3 ♗e6 18 ♕xg6 hxg6 19 ♗e3 led to a favourable two bishop endgame in Tal-Matulovic, Kislovodsk 1966.

c) 10...0-0 11 ♕h5 ♘f6 12 ♕h4 ♕d4 13 ♗g5 ♖d8 14 ♕xd4 ♖xd4 15 ♗d3 b6 16 0-0-0 also gives White the bishop pair in an ending, Gufeld-Khasin, Tallinn 1965.

d) The endgame-loving Ulf Andersson has shown a liking for 10...♘xc3. This is probably the way to play the

position as the alternatives above seem to favour White. Play continues 11 ♗xc3 ♕xd1+ 12 ♖xd1 f6 13 f4 ♗d7 14 ♗c4 (in the game Popovic-Kurajica, Kladovo 1991 White chose a different set-up with 14 ♔f2 0-0-0 15 ♗d3 ♔c7 16 ♖he1 and had similarly strong pressure after 16...♗c8 17 ♖d2 ♘e7 18 ♖de2 ♘d5 19 ♗d2 b6 20 h3 ♔b8 21 g4 etc.) 14...0-0-0 15 0-0

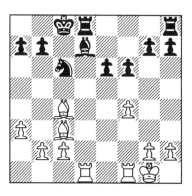

and now:

d1) In Fischer-Addison, New York 1962 Black played the aimless 15...♔c7 and came under strong pressure after 16 ♖de1 ♖he8 17 ♖f3.

d2) 15...♖he8 (Andersson has a regrouping in mind based on establishing a strong-point on d5) 16 b4 ♘e7 17 b5 ♘d5 18 ♗d2 ♘b6 19 ♗d3 ♘a4 20 ♖b1 ♘c5 left Black very well entrenched in Psakhis-Andersson, Manila 1992. Instead of 16 b4, Gallagher suggests 16 ♖de1, preventing ...♘e7 because of the pressure on e6.

10 ♗d3 0-0

After the immediate 10...d4 11 ♘e2 Black has an additional option in 11...♗f5 (11...0-0 leads directly back into the game), though he falls short of equality after 12 0-0 ♗xd3 13 ♕xd3 0-0

14 ♗g5 (14 b4!?, trying to surround d4, has also been played, but the text is much more natural) 14...h6 15 ♗h4 ♖e8 16 ♖ad1 ♖c8 17 c3!? (a far more dynamic treatment than Karpov's 17 ♖fe1, which nevertheless left him slightly better after 17...♖e6 18 ♔f1! ♕c7 19 ♗g3 ♕b6 20 b4 in Karpov-Kuzmin, Leningrad 1977) 17...dxc3 18 ♕h3!? (after 18 ♕f3 ♕e7 19 ♗xf6 ♕xf6 20 ♕xf6 gxf6 21 ♘xc3 it proved very difficult to win in Forster-Boog, Swiss Team Championship 1993) 18...♕e7 19 ♘xc3 ♕e6 20 ♕xe6 fxe6 (20...♖xe6 21 ♗xf6 ♖xf6 22 ♖d7 b6 23 ♖e1 is also unpleasant for Black) 21 ♗xf6 gxf6 22 ♘e4 and White had a clear advantage in the endgame in Estevez-Chaviano, Santa Clara 1983.

11 0-0 d4 12 ♘e2

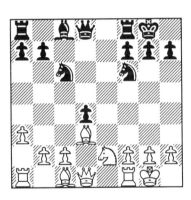

Keeping pieces on the board is a better try for the advantage than 12 ♘e4, after which 12...♗f5 13 ♗g5 ♗xe4 14 ♗xe4 ♕d6 15 ♗xf6 ♕xf6 is rather equal.

12...h6

From Black's point of view this is a major crossroads and the move chosen by Winants may not be Black's best.

a) 12...♗g4 is well met by 13 f3 ♗h5 14 ♗g5 ♕d6 15 ♕e1!, intending ♕f2

and ♖ad1 to put pressure on the d-pawn. Mokry-Stein, Gausdal 1988 continued 15...♗g6 16 ♖d1 ♖fe8 (16...♘d5 17 ♕f2 ♘b6 18 ♗c1! ♖ac8 19 b3 followed by ♗b2 left Black's d-pawn under massive pressure in Topalov-Sion, Leon 1993) 17 ♕f2 ♖ad8 18 ♖d2 ♖d7 (Mokry suggested 18...♖e5 but then 19 ♗h4 intending ♗g3 is strong) 19 ♖fd1 ♖ed8 20 ♗b5! and the d-pawn fell.

b) 12...♕d5 also leaves White better after 13 ♘f4 ♕d6 14 ♘h5 ♘xh5 15 ♕xh5 h6 16 ♖e1 ♗d7 17 ♕h4! (more accurate than preparing ♗f4 with 17 ♕f3 as Black's queen will be unable to go to f6) 17...♖ae8 18 ♗f4 ♕d5 19 ♕g3 ♖e6 20 ♖xe6 ♕xe6 21 ♗d2 ♕e5 22 ♖e1 ♕xg3 23 hxg3 and White had a nice two bishop endgame in Tiviakov-Sorokin, St. Petersburg 1993.

c) 12...♖e8!? is a recent try which intends to meet 13 ♗g5 with 13...♖e5, though it is far from clear how effective this is after 14 ♗h4 (or 14 ♗f4 ♖d5 15 ♗g3!?, intending ♘f4). Wohl-Candelario, Havana 2001 continued 14...♗f5?! (14...♗g4 15 f3 ♗h5 is better) 15 f4 ♖d5 16 ♗xf5 ♖xf5 17 ♘g3 ♖d5 18 ♘e4 ♔h8 19 ♘xf6 gxf6 20 ♕f3 leaving Black with a shattered kingside.

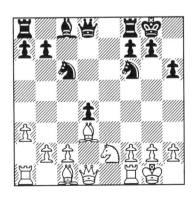

13 ♗f4

The natural move, but with ♗g5 having been prevented, it makes a lot of sense to play 13 b4!?. For example, 13...a6 14 ♗b2 ♔h8 (14...♕d6 15 ♘xd4) and now Black is struggling after Gallagher's suggestion of 15 ♗c4!? (in Petrushin-Bangiev, Simferopol 1989 White played 15 ♕d2 after which 15...♕d6 would have been Black's best).

13...♘d5 14 ♗g3 ♕f6 15 ♖e1 ♘de7 16 ♘f4

Trying to win a pawn with 16 ♘xd4?! ♕xd4 17 ♖xe7 does not work after 17...♗g4 18 ♕d2 ♕xb2 etc.

16...♗f5 17 ♗c4!

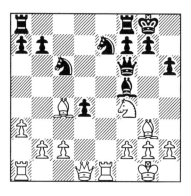

Keeping the bishop pair. 17 ♗xf5 ♕xf5 followed by ...♖ac8 would give Black some pressure against c2.

17...♖ac8 18 ♕d2 ♖fd8 19 ♘d3 ♘g6?!

The knight is not very well placed on this square. Black should play 19...♗g6 followed by ...♘f5 and exchange the bishop on g3 if he can.

20 ♗a2 b6 21 ♗c4?!

Missing the following clever idea by Black. Much simpler and more direct is 21 ♖e2 followed by 22 ♖ae1, when White's position remains somewhat preferable.

21...♘b8!

Well played! Black prevents the bishop from coming to a6 and routes the knight towards c5 via d7. Objectively speaking the position is now equal.

22 b3 ♘d7 23 ♖e2 ♘c5 24 ♖ae1 a6 25 ♘xc5 ♖xc5 26 ♖e8+ ♖xe8 27 ♖xe8+ ♔h7 28 h4??

A time-trouble blunder, giving away a pawn for nothing. Fortunately for Geller, and perhaps worried that he might have missed something, his opponent does not take it.

28...b5!

Exactly. The immediate 28...♘xh4?! is met by 29 ♗xh4 ♕xh4 30 ♗xf7 ♖xc2 31 ♕e1 when Black has to defend against the threat of 32 ♖h8+. But now the bishop is unable to maintain its pressure against f7.

29 ♗d3 ♕c6??

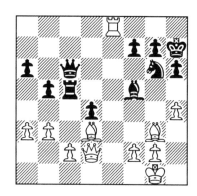

Turning a very good position into a lost one. Simply 29...♘xh4! leaves Black a pawn up for nothing.

30 ♖d8 ♗xd3 31 ♕xd3 h5 32 ♖d6 ♕c8 33 ♕xd4 ♖xc2 34 ♕d5!

The winning move, forking f5 and h5.

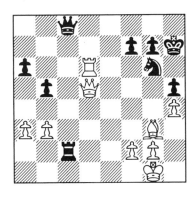

34...♕g4 35 ♕xf7 ♘xh4 36 ♖d8 ♖c1+ 37 ♔h2 ♘f5 38 ♕g8+ ♔g6 39 ♕e8+ ♔h7 40 ♕g8+ ♔g6 41 ♖a8 ♕e4 42 ♖xa6+ ♖c6 43 f3 1-0

Game 49
Al.Ivanov-Gufeld
USSR 1983

---

1 e4 c5 2 ♘f3 ♘c6 3 d4 cxd4 4 ♘xd4 ♕b6

4...♘f6 5 ♘c3 ♕b6 transposes back into the game. Nimzowitsch once played 4...d5 but this leads to an advantage for White after 5 ♘xc6 bxc6 6 exd5 ♕xd5 (6...cxd5 7 ♗b5+ wins a pawn) 7 ♘d2 ♘f6 8 ♗e2 e6 9 0-0 ♗e7 10 ♗f3 ♕d6 11 ♕e2, followed by 12 ♘c4 (or

even 11 ♘c4 immediately).

5 ♘b3 ♘f6 6 ♘c3 e6 7 g3 ♗b4

The only move of independent significance. 7...d6 would lead to positions akin to the Scheveningen Variation but with Black losing some time with his queen after ♗c1-e3.

8 ♗g2 d5 9 0-0

Another possibility is 9 exd5 ♘xd5 10 0-0!, after which T.Cooper-Olthof, Philadelphia 1990 continued 10...♘xc3 11 bxc3 ♗xc3 12 ♖b1 (it may also be worth investigating 12 ♗a3!? ♗xa1 13 ♕xa1 f6 14 ♕d1, intending ♕h5+) 12...0-0 13 ♕f3 ♗f6 14 ♗e3 ♕c7 15 ♘c5 with compensation for the pawn.

9...♗xc3 10 bxc3

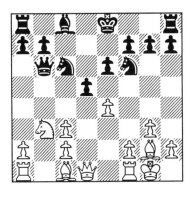

A much calmer possibility is 10 exd5, after which 10...♘xd5 11 bxc3 ♘xc3 is bad because of 12 ♕g4!. Ivanov's choice leads to a very sharp game.

10...♘xe4 11 ♕g4

White should avoid 11 ♗xe4 dxe4 12 ♕g4 as after 12...♗d7 13 ♕xg7 0-0-0 his light squares would be weak.

11...♗d7

Counterattack! After 11...g6 I think that 12 c4 is very promising due to the severe weakness of Black's dark squares.

12 ♕xg7 0-0-0 13 c4

After 13 ♗e3 ♕b5 White would be unable to arrange this move.

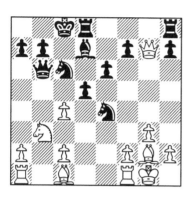

13...♖hg8 14 ♕b2 ♘xg3! 15 hxg3 ♖xg3 16 ♗e3

Readers with some time on their hands may care to analyse the consequences of 16 c5!? ♖xg2+ 17 ♔xg2 ♕b4 (17...♖g8+ 18 ♔f3! lets White's king escape) 18 ♕g7!?, when it is far from clear that Black is compensated for his rook.

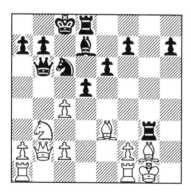

16...♖xg2+

16...♖dg8?! is bad because of 17 fxg3 (and not 17 ♗xb6 ♖xg2+ 18 ♔h1 ♖2g5 followed by 19...♖h5 mate) 17...♕xe3+ 18 ♖f2. On the other hand, it is worth considering 16...♖xe3!? 17 fxe3 dxc4 18 ♕c3 cxb3 with compensation for the exchange.

17 ♔xg2 d4!

18 ♗f4

And not 18 ♗xd4? ♘xd4 19 ♕xd4 ♗c6+ etc.

18...e5! 19 ♗g3 ♘e7 20 ♕a3 ♕c6+?

A slip. In his notes Gufeld recommended 20...♕h6, when Black has compensation after 21 ♖h1 ♗c6+ 22 f3 ♕e3 etc.

21 f3 ♘f5 22 ♔f2??

In this wild position it is no surprise that both players should make errors. White can simply play 22 ♕xa7! as 22...♖g8 is answered by 23 ♕a8+.

22...♘xg3 23 ♔xg3 ♕h6!

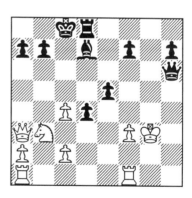

24 ♕c1

White's king is in a net. If 24 ♕c5+ there follows 24...♗c6 25 ♕xe5 ♖g8+ 26 ♔f2 ♕h4+ 27 ♔e2 ♖e8 winning the queen.

24...♖g8+ 25 ♔f2 ♕h2+ 26 ♔e1 ♖g2 27 ♘d2 ♗a4 28 ♖b1 d3

Black could win most simply with 28...♖e2+ 29 ♔d1 ♕g2 30 ♖b4 d3 31 ♖xa4 ♖xd2+ 32 ♕xd2 ♕xf1+ 33 ♕e1 dxc2+ etc. The text doesn't spoil anything but it is far messier.

29 ♖b3 ♖e2+ 30 ♔d1 ♖e3??

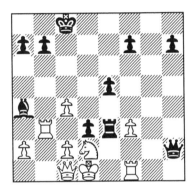

Missing the last chance of victory. Black can still put the ball away with 30...♗xb3 31 axb3 ♕g2 32 cxd3 ♖xd2+ 33 ♕xd2 ♕xf1+ 34 ♔c2 ♕xf3 with a winning queen and pawn endgame.

31 cxd3 ½-½

Game 50
Velickovic-Mnatsakanian
Tbilisi 1983

---

1 e4 c5 2 ♘f3

The Nimzowitsch Variation, with which Black provokes White's e-pawn to advance in the style of Alekhine's Defence.

2...♘f6 3 e5 ♘d5 4 g3!?

Once again White's bishop comes to the g2-square, from where it bears down on the h1-a8 diagonal and helps White control the centre. It can be seen as an improved form of Rozentalis' 1 e4 c5 2 c3 ♘f6 3 e5 ♘d5 4 g3, in which White has played ♘g1-f3 rather than c2-c3. The main line is 4 ♘c3, after which 4...e6 5 ♘xd5 exd5 6 d4 ♘c6 7 dxc5 ♗xc5 8 ♕xd5 ♕b6 gives Black some compensation in a position with many tricks. I consider it quite impractical to debate the intricacies of such variations with a specialist, when there are good alternatives available.

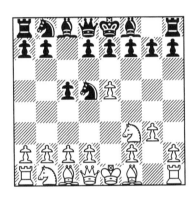

4...d6

Immediately undermining e5 like this must surely be Black's most logical choice, but there are a number of alternatives:

a) 4...e6 lets White maintain a nice space advantage with 5 ♗g2 d6 6 0-0 ♘c6 7 exd6 ♗xd6 8 d4 0-0 (8...cxd4 9 ♘xd4 0-0 10 ♘xc6 bxc6 11 c4 ♘e7 12 ♘c3 ♖b8 13 b3 ♗e5 14 ♕e1 f6 15 ♗e3 was nice for White in R.Byrne-Regan, US Championship, Pasadena 1978) 9 dxc5 ♗xc5 10 ♘bd2 ♗e7 (after 10...b5 White should play 11 ♘b3 ♗e7 12 c3 followed by ♕e2) 11 ♕e2 ♕c7 12 ♘b3 b5 13 c3 a6 14 ♗g5 h6 15 ♗xe7 ♘cxe7

16 ♘e5 and White had an edge in Popovic-Yang Xian, Dubai 1986.

b) 4...♘c6 5 ♗g2 ♕c7 attacks the e-pawn (after 5...g6 6 0-0 ♗g7 7 d4 cxd4 8 ♘xd4 White maintains a nice space advantage), but White can sacrifice it with 6 0-0. In Popovic-Bjelajac, Novi Sad 1981 White obtained very strong play after 6...♘xe5 7 ♘xe5 ♕xe5 8 d4! cxd4 9 ♖e1 ♕d6 and now 10 ♕xd4! (in the game White played 10 ♘a3!? which was far less clear) 10...♕b4 11 ♕d1 would leave White just one pawn down but with a massive lead in development.

c) 4...b6 5 ♗g2 ♗a6 6 d3 ♘c6 7 0-0 e6 8 ♖e1 ♗e7 9 c4 ♘c7 10 b3 0-0 was Popovic-Shirazi, New York 1986. This seems nice for White after 11 ♗b2 (in the game White lost control after 11 d4 cxd4 12 ♘xd4 ♘xd4 13 ♕xd4 d5 14 exd6 ♗f6 15 ♕f4 ♘d5 16 cxd5 ♗xa1 etc.).

5 ♗g2 ♘c6 6 exd6 ♕xd6 7 0-0 ♗g4

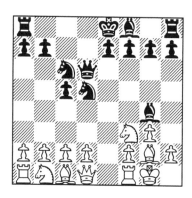

The other way to prevent 8 d4 is with 7...e5, but the danger here is that Black's centre is very exposed. In Popovic-Ivanovic, Belgrade 1987 White maintained an initiative with 8 ♘a3 ♘b6 9 ♘b5 ♕d7 10 ♖e1 ♗e7 11 a4 f6 12 c3 a6 13 ♘a3 ♕d8 14 d4 cxd4 15 cxd4 ♗g4

16 h3 ♗h5 17 ♘c2 ♖c8 18 b3 0-0 19 ♗b2 ♘b4 20 ♘xb4 ♗xb4 21 dxe5 ♗xe1 22 ♕xe1 ♗xf3 23 ♗xf3 fxe5 24 ♕xe5 with more than enough compensation for the sacrificed exchange.

8 h3

The immediate 8 ♘c3 is also possible, but it makes sense to interpolate the moves 8 h3 ♗h5 so as to have the possibility of breaking the pin on the f3-knight with a later g3-g4.

8...♗h5

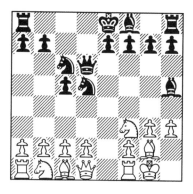

9 d4!

White did not repeat Velickovic's treatment in later games, though as Black's choice of opening probably came as a surprise, it would be unlikely that players had studied existing theory beforehand. In Shabalov-Christiansen, US Championship, Parsippany 1996 White nevertheless gained the advantage with 9 ♘c3, after which 9...♘xc3 10 bxc3 e6 11 ♖b1 ♕c7 12 d4 ♖d8 13 ♕e2 cxd4 14 g4 d3 15 cxd3 ♗g6 16 ♘d4 ♘xd4 17 cxd4 gave him a powerful initiative.

9...♗xf3

Both 9...♘xd4 10 g4 ♗g6 11 ♘xd4 cxd4 12 ♕xd4 and 9...cxd4 10 g4 ♗g6 11 ♘xd4 ♘db4 12 ♘xc6! are very good for White. Black's best chance may be 9...0-0-0!?, after which 10 c4 ♘b6 11 d5 ♘xc4 (11...e6 12 ♘c3 exd5 13 ♗f4 leaves Black's king very exposed) 12 ♘c3 gives White good compensation for his pawn, but things are by no means crystal clear.

10 ♕xf3 e6 11 dxc5 ♕xc5 12 ♘c3!?

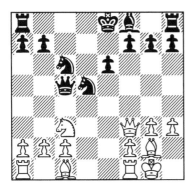

A dynamic interpretation of the position, accepting doubled c-pawns in order to accelerate White's development and open the b-file. A good alternative is the simple 12 c3.

12...♘xc3 13 bxc3 ♗e7 14 ♖b1 ♘d8

The only way to defend b7 as after 14...♖b8? there is 15 ♖xb7!. The drawback is that Black is now very passive.

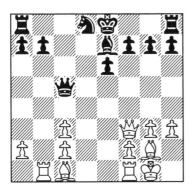

15 ♖d1 0-0 16 ♖b3

Not bad, but 16 ♖d7! would have been more incisive.

16...♕c7 17 ♕f4!

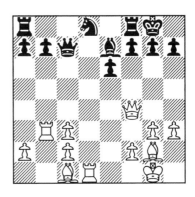

17...e5

After the exchange of queens White's rook would come to d7 with deadly effect. Therefore Black is forced to weaken himself further, the text opening up light squares for White's bishop on g2.

18 ♕f5 ♗d6 19 ♕d3 ♗c5 20 ♕f5

Once again the seventh rank is key, and with 20 ♕d7! White would gain a well nigh winning position.

20...♗d6

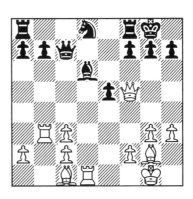

21 ♗e4?

White is starting to lose the plot – he

should not be attempting to attack on the kingside. White can still retrace his steps with 21 ♕d3 ♗e7 22 ♕d7 etc.

21...g6 22 ♕f3 ♖b8 23 ♕d3 ♗c5?

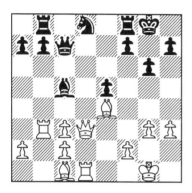

Missing a golden opportunity to equalise with 23...♘e6!, the point being that 24 ♕xd6?? loses to 24...♖fd8. Now White finally takes the right path.

24 ♕d7! ♕xd7 25 ♖xd7 ♗b6 26 ♗a3 ♖e8 27 c4 ♖c8 28 ♗d5 e4 29 ♔f1! ♘e6

Black has run out of good moves. 29...♔g7 is met by 30 ♔e2 followed by ♖b5 and c5.

30 ♖xb7 ♘c7 31 ♗c6 ♖e5 32 c5 ♗xc5 33 ♗d7 ♗xa3 34 ♖xa3 1-0

Game 51
Lalic-Davies
Southend 2000

---

1 e4 c5 2 ♘f3 e6 3 ♘c3

This is quite a good move order against 2...e6. By delaying d2-d4 White avoids having to swot up variations such as 3 d4 cxd4 4 ♘xd4 ♘f6 5 ♘c3 ♗b4 6 e5, which may be good for White but is very complicated. Some players specialise in lines like this and know of many wrinkles that have been

neglected by mainstream theory. In my opinion it is not a practical proposition to take them on in their own back yards.

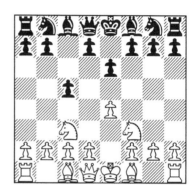

3...a6 4 g3 b5 5 d4 b4 6 ♘a4 ♗b7

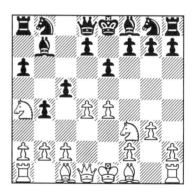

Over-the-board improvisation, which was an attempt to avoid the main lines of theory. Unfortunately Lalic was more than equal to the task and he obtains a very strong position out of the opening. 6...cxd4 7 ♘xd4 leads to the lines considered in Chapter 5.

7 ♘xc5! ♗xc5 8 dxc5 ♗xe4 9 ♗g2 ♘f6 10 0-0 0-0 11 ♖e1 ♘c6 12 ♗f4 ♕a5

White's 14th move shows that this is not a good square for the queen. 12...h6 might have been a better try.

13 ♗d6 ♖fc8 14 a3 ♗d5 15 axb4 ♕xb4 16 b3 ♘e8?

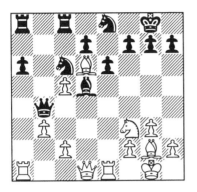

Moving the knight away from the kingside has very serious consequences. Perhaps I should have played 16...a5 but then 17 ♖a4 ♕b7 18 c4 ♗xf3 19 ♗xf3 leaves Black with rather grizzly prospects.

17 ♖a4 ♕b7 18 ♘g5! ♘f6

After 18...♗xg2 comes 19 ♕h5.

19 ♗xd5 exd5 20 ♖f4! ♖e8 21 ♖xe8+ ♖xe8 22 ♘xf7! d4

Obviously I did not want to allow my opponent the gold coins that would follow after 22...♔xf7 23 ♕h5+ ♔g8 (23...♔e6 24 ♖xf6+) 24 ♕xe8+ ♘xe8 25 ♖f8 mate.

23 ♖xf6 d3

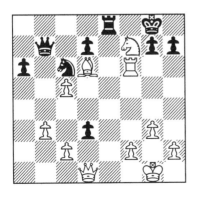

An attempt to make room for the king so as to improve on the variation after 23...gxf6 when White plays the continuation 24 ♕g4+ ♔xf7 25 ♕h5+ ♔e6 26 ♕xe8+. However, White quite rightly ignores it.

24 ♘h6+ gxh6 25 ♕g4+ ♔h8 26 ♖f8+ ♖xf8 27 ♗xf8 d6 28 ♗xd6 dxc2 29 ♕c4 ♕xb3 30 ♕xb3 c1♕+

Despite my best efforts at stirring up some trouble, the position is still quite lost.

31 ♔g2 ♕e1 32 ♕f7 ♕e4+ 33 f3 ♕c2+ 34 ♔h3 ♕g6 35 ♕d7 ♕h5+ 36 ♔g2 ♕d5 37 ♕c8+ ♔g7 38 ♕xa6 h5 39 ♕e2 h4 40 g4 h5 41 ♔h3 hxg4+ 42 ♔xg4 ♔f7 43 ♕e4 1-0

Game 52
Shamkovich-Marchand
USA 1977

1 e4 c5 2 ♘f3 a6

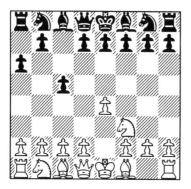

The O'Kelly Variation, which is much better than its reputation. From our point of view it requires special attention because Black can prevent us from reaching the desired set-up with g2-g3.

Another variation which forces White to change tack is Katalymov's 2...b6, after which 3 d4 cxd4 4 ♘xd4 ♗b7 5 ♘c3 e6 should be met by 6 ♘db5 (6 g3 ♗b4 is disturbing). Then 6...d6 7 ♗f4 e5 8 ♗e3 a6 9 ♘a3 b5 10 ♘d5 ♘d7 11 c4 is better for White.

3 ♘c3!

The main point of the O'Kelly is that after 3 d4 Black can play 3...cxd4 4 ♘xd4 ♘f6 5 ♘c3 e5 with a kind of Najdorf in which Black has the option of playing ...♗b4. Most books recommend either 3 c3 or 3 c4, but against 3 c4 Black can play 3...♘c6 4 d4 cxd4 5 ♘xd4 e5 6 ♘f5 d6 7 ♘c3 g6 8 ♘e3 ♗g7 followed by ...♘ge7 and ...0-0 with very reasonable play. After 3 c3 it is interest-

ing to transpose into an unusual line of the Advance French with 3...e6 4 d4 d5 5 e5 ♗d7, intending to exchange the light-squared bishops with 6...♗b5.

3...b5 4 d4 cxd4 5 ♘xd4 ♗b7 6 ♗g5!?

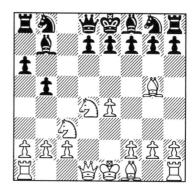

With Black having fianchettoed his bishop so early, this position calls for White to change track. After 6 g3? Black has 6...b4 7 ♘d5 e6 winning the e4-pawn.

6...♕a5!?

As Shamkovich pointed out, both 6...♘f6 7 ♗xf6 gxf6 8 ♕h5 and 6...♕c7 7 ♘d5 ♗xd5 (or 7...♕e5 8 ♗e3) 8 exd5 ♕e5+ 9 ♗e3 ♕xd5 10 ♗e2, threatening ♗f3, give White the advantage.

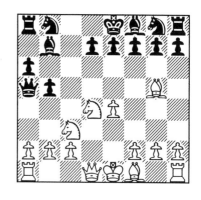

7 ♘b3 ♕b6 8 ♗e2 e6 9 0-0 b4?!

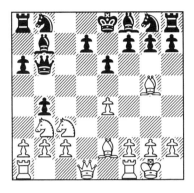

Attempting to exploit the lack of co-ordination in White's forces, yet it proves to be far too risky because of Black's lagging development. He should try to develop his pieces, say with 9...♘c6. Now he falls victim to a most beautifully conceived attack.

10 ♘a4! ♕c6 11 ♘a5 ♕xa4 12 ♘xb7 ♕c6 13 ♘d8!!

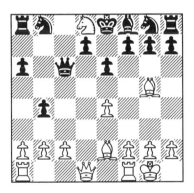

A most extraordinary move, the knight stealing into the deepest part of the enemy camp in order to unlock the gates for White's other pieces. Black was probably banking on 13 ♘a5 ♕c5 (forking knight and bishop), after which White has to resort to 14 ♗d8! ♘c6 15 ♘xc6 dxc6 16 ♗h4 ♘f6 with a fairly equal game.

13...♕c7 14 ♗h5! g6 15 ♕f3

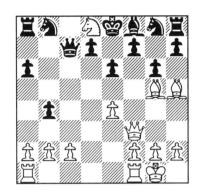

15...d6

As Shamkovich pointed out, 15...f6 would have been a more stubborn defence. White should then play 16 e5! ♕xd8 (after 16...♔xd8 there is 17 ♗xf6+ ♘xf6 18 ♕xf6+ ♔e8 19 ♗f3; or if 16...gxh5 White wins with 17 exf6 ♔xd8 18 f7+ ♔c8 19 ♕xa8 ♘e7 20 ♗f6 etc.) 17 exf6 ♔f7 18 ♖ad1 ♘c6 (18...gxh5 19 ♕xh5 mate) 19 ♖fe1 ♘xf6 20 ♗g4 with a strong attack for the sacrificed piece.

16 ♗g4

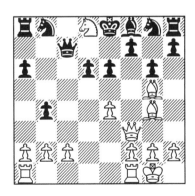

Threatening 17 ♗xe6 fxe6 18 ♕xf8+, winning a piece. Black's necessary defensive measures create new weaknesses.

16...h6 17 ♗h4 ♗g7

After 17...g5 there follows 18 ♘xf7 ♕xf7 19 ♗h5 etc.

18 e5 d5 19 ♗xe6! fxe6 20 ♘xe6 ♕b7 21 ♘xg7+ ♕xg7 22 ♕xd5

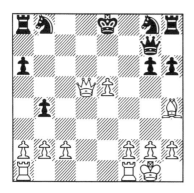

Utter devastation.

22...♕a7 23 ♖ad1 g5 24 e6 ♔f8 25 ♕f3+ 1-0

The finish would be 25 ♕f3+ ♔e8 (or 25...♔g7 26 ♖d7+) 26 ♕h5+ ♔f8 27 ♖d8+ ♔g7 28 ♖d7+, winning.

Summary

Most of the lines in this chapter are quite playable, but none of them has the same pedigree as more recognised variations. The Four Knights is rather passive, 4...♕b6 will lose some time with the queen, whilst the Nimzowitsch and O'Kelly Variations bend the rules of development and leave Black skating on very thin ice.

Needless to say, all these lines can become very effective should White play inaccurately or passively. As this is precisely how many players react when they are surprised in the opening, the reader would be well advised to take each of these lines quite seriously. If you know exactly what to do their surprise value will be eradicated and the real value of these openings can be tested.

INDEX OF VARIATIONS

The Najdorf Variation

1 e4 c5 2 ♘f3 d6 3 d4 cxd4 4 ♘xd4 ♘f6 5 ♘c3 a6 6 g3 e5 7 ♘de2 b5 8 ♗g2 ♗b7 9 0-0 ♗e7 10 h3 ♘bd7 11 g4

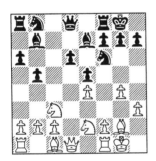

11...b4
  11...0-0 12 ♘g3 ♘c5
    13 ♗e3 *17*; 13 f4 *19*
12 ♘d5 ♘xd5 13 exd5 0-0
  13...a5 *14*; 13...h5 *15*
14 ♘g3 g6 *10*
  14...♖e8 *13*

The Classical Variation

1 e4 c5 2 ♘f3 d6 3 d4 cxd4 4 ♘xd4 ♘f6 5 ♘c3 ♘c6 6 g3 e5
  6...♕b6 *33*; 6...♘xd4 *36*; 6...a6 *31*
  6...♗g4 7 f3 ♗d7 8 ♗e3

        8...e6 *23*; 8...g6 *25*

7 ♘de2 ♗e7 *27*

7....♗g4 *30*

The Scheveningen Variation

1 e4 c5 2 ♘f3 d6 3 d4 cxd4 4 ♘xd4 ♘f6 5 ♘c3 e6 6 g3 a6

      6...♘c6 7 ♗g2 ♗d7 8 0-0

          8...a6 *52*; 8....♗e7 *54*

7 ♗g2 ♕c7 8 0-0

8...♗e7

      8...♘c6 *48*

9 f4

      9 ♗e3 *45*; 9 a4 *43*

9...0-0 10 g4 ♘c6 11 ♘xc6 bxc6 12 g5 ♘e8 13 ♗e3 *40*

      13 ♔h1 *41*

Paulsen and Taimanov Variations

1 e4 c5 2 ♘f3 e6 3 d4 cxd4 4 ♘xd4 ♘c6 5 ♘c3 ♕c7

      5...a6 6 g3 ♘ge7 *69*

6 g3 a6 7 ♗g2

The Kan Variation

The Pelikan-Sveshnikov Variation

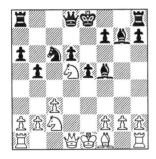

Löwenthal, Kalashnikov and other ...e7-e5 Lines

5...d6 *97*

6 ♘d6+ ♗xd6 7 ♕xd6 ♕f6 8 ♕xf6 ♘xf6 9 ♘c3 ♘b4 *100*

9...d5 *102*

Dragons

1 e4 c5 2 ♘f3 d6

2...♘c6 3 d4 cxd4 4 ♘xd4 g6 5 ♘c3 ♗g7 6 ♘de2 d6 7 g3 *121*

3 d4 cxd4 4 ♘xd4 ♘f6 5 ♘c3 g6 6 g3 ♘c6 7 ♘de2

7...♗g7

7...b6 *108*; 7...♗d7 *111*

8 ♗g2 0-0 9 0-0 ♖b8

9...♗d7 *112*

10 a4 a6 *119*

10...b6 *116*

Other Lines

1 e4 c5 2 ♘f3 ♘c6

2...♘f6 *131*; 2...a6 *136*

2...e6 3 ♘c3 a6 4 g3 b5 5 d4 b4 6 ♘a4 ♗b7 *134*

3 d4 cxd4 4 ♘xd4 ♘f6

4...♕b6 *129*

5 ♘c3 e6 6 ♘db5 *125*

INDEX OF COMPLETE GAMES